T0330777

ROUTLEDGE LIBRARY EDITIONS:
SOVIET ECONOMICS

Volume 2

THE COMMUNIST ECONOMIC
CHALLENGE

THE COMMUNIST ECONOMIC CHALLENGE

DAVID INGRAM

Routledge
Taylor & Francis Group

LONDON AND NEW YORK

First published in 1965 by George Allen & Unwin

This edition first published in 2023
by Routledge
4 Park Square, Milton Park, Abingdon, Oxon OX14 4RN

and by Routledge
605 Third Avenue, New York, NY 10158

Routledge is an imprint of the Taylor & Francis Group, an informa business

© 1965 David Ingram

British Library Cataloguing in Publication Data
A catalogue record for this book is available from the British Library

ISBN: 978-1-032-48466-2 (Set)
ISBN: 978-1-032-49334-3 (Volume 2) (hbk)
ISBN: 978-1-032-49339-8 (Volume 2) (pbk)
ISBN: 978-1-003-39331-3 (Volume 2) (ebk)

DOI: 10.4324/9781003393313

Publisher's Note
The publisher has gone to great lengths to ensure the quality of this reprint but points out that some imperfections in the original copies may be apparent.

Disclaimer
The publisher has made every effort to trace copyright holders and would welcome correspondence from those they have been unable to trace.

THE COMMUNIST
ECONOMIC CHALLENGE

BY
DAVID INGRAM

London
GEORGE ALLEN & UNWIN LTD

PRINTED IN GREAT BRITAIN
in 10 point Times Roman
BY SIMSON SHAND LTD
LONDON, HERTFORD AND HARLOW

CONTENTS

CHAPTER I

Introduction

This book is about the economic achievements and potentialities of Communism. A general awareness of the military might of the Soviet Union and the kind of political ambition it supports has existed since the end of the Second World War, but it is only in the last ten years or so that attention has been properly focused on the economic threat. In particular, the much-vaunted, and indeed spectacular launching of the Soviet sputnik in 1957 plunged many people in the West into gloom, for it seemed to demonstrate a level of economic development and technical accomplishment above the average estimate and, in some ways, far in advance of our own. This readjustment of thinking had followed a significant reappraisal of policy within the Communist world. The maintenance of a rough balance of military power had largely contained the expansion of communism by brute force, but had certainly not sapped its dynamism. The era of 'peaceful co-existence' has also been the age of 'peaceful competition'. On the one hand, the Communist powers realized after the Korean war that a frontal attack on the positions of other countries was precluded by the promise of retaliation but, at the same time, the completion of postwar reconstruction in the bloc meant that they now felt more able to challenge the West with economic weapons. New territories were not to be gained by physical force, but by such means as the emulation of the Communist way of life. This policy has fully flowered with the rise of Khrushchev. It is Khrushchev who insists that the two opposing systems are engaged in an economic race: 'let the nations contend' is his slogan. Peaceful co-existence, in fact, is the continuation of the class war by other means.

For Communist leaders themselves there is little doubt about the outcome of the conflict, be it waged by military or economic means. Time, they think, is on their side and the inexorable working out of

those immutable historical laws discovered by Marx and Lenin
ensure the final victory. In a speech at Vlore in Albania in 1959,
Khrushchev was typically optimistic:

'Communism is the cherished long awaited dream of the working
people, the bright future of humanity. And no matter how decrepit
capitalism tries to prolong its existence, it is doomed, for a new
victorious system, communism, is coming along to take its place.
This is life, comrades; everyone of you knows that however strong a
man may be, in time he becomes senile and his last day comes
regardless of what medicine he takes. No medicine will help a dying
organism; thus, no medicine will help capitalism. We must do
everything not to delay the process.'

It was during his visit to the United States in the same year that
Khrushchev made that notorious aside about 'burying capitalism',
but what he really meant was that it would surely dig its own grave.
According to Communist canons, world capitalism has recently
entered a new, third stage of its general crisis. This epoch is character-
ized by 'the upsurge of the national liberation movement' and 'the
breaking up of the colonial system'. The contradictions and
antagonisms in the capitalist camp, both between the States themselves in their competition for markets and between the various
classes in each country, are increasing as, of course, is the exploitation and impoverishment of the working masses. Simultaneously, the
'Socialist countries are winning one position after another from the
old world, raising their share of global output, and outstripping
everyone else in rates of economic development'.

For the faithful this is an appealingly simple and comforting
picture, but the claims of superiority for the Communist system and
evidence of the impending downfall of capitalism are presented with
such confidence and so amply supported by factual and statistical
data that they have impressed many other people too. Until recently,
the image of Communist progress that existed in the minds of many
citizens of the West had differed little from what Khrushchev had
wanted it to be. The belief that east of the Iron Curtain were millions
of men and women, toiling ceaselessly under near-military discipline
to outproduce and defeat us economically was common. It had also
been thought that the day was not far off when the Communist world
would be in a position to deluge the markets of the world with
products as various as strawberry pulp and crude petroleum, rob us
of our markets and generally disrupt our economies.

These impressions were formed regardless of whether the ordinary person read or listened to Communist propaganda. For the most part it is directly attributable to reading his own organs of news and opinion. This is not due to the hidden hand of Communism but because of the special nature of what is almost the only available information on Sino-Soviet affairs. Political and economic correspondents, whether reporting on East or West, must rely heavily on official statements; in the case of Communist countries it is the official hand-out or virtually nothing at all. This information is deliberately slanted to create the best propaganda effect, and most of the correspondents know it. But it takes a discerning and well-informed mind to discover quickly how much truth there is in these statements. They are usually long and complex and, more often than not, take considerable time to analyse—far too long to suit the demands of editors anxious to meet a deadline. All this is especially true of information on economic matters where a correct interpretation often depends on an abstruse technical definition. There was a time when the majority of Soviet pronouncements could safely be regarded as worthless propaganda and be given little or no attention in the West. But since the death of Stalin, the USSR has realized that it has made real progress in spheres where its purpose is served by being neither mendacious nor secretive, and western observers have learned the dangers of disbelieving or ignoring Soviet announcements. In any case, by virtue of Khrushchev's personal showmanship and because of the mystery which still shrouds much of the Soviet scene, its affairs are news in much the same way as were those of Hitler's Germany. Whether we like it or not, we are all in danger of being mesmerized.

Anyone who has time to make a careful study of the affairs of the Communist world is not likely to be impressed by the published information. The more closely he examines the official Press and broadcasts and delves into the technical and learned periodicals as well as into the daily newspapers, he will probably reach different conclusions from any formed through a more hasty approach. He will realize that, while the USSR and China and their allies are undoubtedly making rapid progress, they face difficulties far greater than they have admitted, and that it is by no means proven that the final triumph belongs to the Communist system, or even that it provides the most satisfactory answer to humanity's problems. Indeed, it is arguable that there is more danger from an uncritical western acceptance of Communist claims to superiority than there is from the intrinsic power of the Communist world.

This book tries to take advantage of an unhurried approach to get as close as possible to the real facts about the Communist economies and to assess Communist attempts to make an economic impact on the rest of the world. It should then be easier to see more clearly what kind of challenge confronts us. Since the Communist leaders resort so liberally to comparisons with other countries, and since yardsticks are needed with which to judge Communist economic developments, this book will itself make frequent use of such measurements.

The treatment of Chinese developments is rather more historical than that applied to the other Communist countries. This is largely because of the nature of the available data, which are both scarce and, where official statistics are concerned, much less reliable than those of the USSR and Communist Eastern Europe. Over the past three years in particular there has been a virtual blackout in Chinese statistics. The only way in which to form any kind of picture of the economy in such a situation is to use the fragments of up-to-date information available in a historical setting. In other words, each scrap has to be fitted on to the more reliable knowledge acquired on earlier developments, thereby providing a foundation for an assessment. This approach, which was also the only one possible for the USSR during the last years of Stalin, has certain advantages. As one of the most recent examples of an under-developed country trying to modernize and expand its production by Communist methods China merits as detailed an examination as possible.

Though most of this book deals with economic matters, attention must also be given to defence expenditure. This is because today such expenditure is usually high enough to exercise a considerable influence on economic development. It is generally accepted that Soviet defence expenditure is among the heaviest in the world, but no one is quite sure how heavy it really is; few are disposed to think it is what the Soviet authorities say it is. Some light is shed on this question in the contexts of both the competition between the USSR and USA in the production of modern armaments and space vehicles, and of the burden such activities must impose on the economy of a country whose leaders seek to lead the world economically as well as militarily.

CHAPTER II

The World Balance Sheet

What is the economic balance sheet of the opposing forces in the present global conflict? According to official Soviet figures, the struggle has, in terms of territory and population, developed since 1919 as follows:

	'Socialist Camp'		'Imperialist Capitalist Camp'*		Rest of World	
	1919	End 1962	1919	End 1962	1919	End 1962
Area						
Million sq. kilometres	21.7	35.2	60.3	15.0	53.2	85.0
Per cent	16.0	26.1	44.5	11.1	39.5	62.8
Population						
Millions	138.0	1112	855	524.3	784.0	1513.7
Per cent	7.8	35.3	48.1	16.6	44.1	48.1

* USA, UK, West Germany, France, Japan, Italy, and their Colonies.

Thus, at the end of 1962, the area and population under Communist rule were both more than double those under the rule of Communism's opponents whereas, only forty-three years earlier, the balance had been overwhelmingly in favour of the latter. The vast majority of the 974 million people who have been won for Communism since 1919 had little say in the matter; the 13 million square kilometres of territory they inhabit was mainly acquired by annexation, civil war and subversion.

The vast areas and populations of the uncommitted countries, which in large part constitute the 'under-developed world', could exist, according to the Communists, be the victims of imperialist exploitation but for their own national awakening and the sympathy and support of the Communist world. In fact many are considered ripe for revolution. What is not disputed is that these uncommitted countries include most of the poorest peoples of the world. Their populations are increasing fast and their only hope of material betterment lies in a development of their human and material resources. In spite of their poverty (indeed, partly because of it), they are of great political significance in the modern world, and perhaps the most important battleground in the ideological struggle between East and West.

Area and population is one thing, relative economic strength is another. Just how strong are the economies of the Communist countries in relation to those of the countries to which their leaders choose to be opposed? How great is the poverty of the uncommitted countries? Unfortunately, there is no really accurate measuring rod. Gross National Product (GNP), which is a yearly calculation of the physical volume of goods and services produced by an economy expressed in value terms, is a useful concept when applied to a single country, but innumerable difficulties arise when GNP comparisons are made between one nation and another. Any two economies are as different as chalk and cheese. The price structures and patterns of consumption are dissimilar; there are thorny problems of weighting and realistic exchange rates. The normal difficulties of comparison are multiplied when it comes to Communist countries which do not publish the kind of GNP statistics familiar in the West and often conceal information that would aid an independent estimate. It is possible, however, to form rough orders of magnitude. In 1963, for instance, it is estimated that the GNP (reckoned in market prices and in dollars) of the Communist world, with its 1,100 million population, was at least some 20 per cent less than that of the USA with a population of 193 million.

More realistic indicators are found in the statistical volumes of the United Nations and similar publications. These give figures not only of population but of the output and consumption of a number of important products in nearly every country of the world. Some of these, notably crude steel output, primary energy consumption and grain output, when considered together, speak volumes about an economy. In all but a few countries, crude steel output is a fairly good indicator of total industrial capacity, particularly that of the engineering industries which, with shipbuilding, construction and railways, are the main consumers of steel. An even better indicator than crude steel output would be annual consumption (output plus imports minus exports) of finished steel. Unfortunately, this can only be calculated for a few countries. For world-wide comparisons, we must be satisfied with the output of crude steel, which is one of the most easily and accurately measurable of all products.

Primary energy consumption can often rectify the picture of a country whose crude steel output is misleading, although neither of them is a particularly good indicator of activity in the textile, clothing, and other consumer goods industries which are important in such highly developed regions as the USA and Western Europe, and relatively even more important in some of the least developed. In the United Nations statistics, primary energy consumption is taken to comprise annual output plus imports minus exports of coal, brown coal, crude petroleum, natural gas and hydro-electricity expressed in terms of hard coal. Peat, wood, dung, and other such fuels have proved impossible to cover; they are of little importance in the more developed countries but significant in the poorer ones.

Grain production, the most doubtful of all the indicators, is extremely hard to assess, particularly in peasant communities. Although it is consumed by animals as well as humans and is therefore relevant to the output of meat and dairy produce, grain and its animal derivatives are by no means the only major items of human food consumption. Its virtue lies in its having the highest quality among vegetable products in relation to its weight, and it is, therefore, the best single indicator of agricultural production as a whole. Like energy consumption, it tends to exaggerate the poverty of the poorer countries, whose output cannot be accurately assessed and which in any case rely heavily on vegetable foodstuffs other than grain. With their limitations in mind, the indicators can now be examined.

A number of important facts are brought out by this table. To begin with, let us confine comparisons to the Communist economies on the one hand and those of the English-speaking countries, Western Europe, and Japan on the other. By 1961 or thereabouts, the population of the former outnumbered that of the latter by as much as 70 per cent, but the industries of the non-Communist group were at least twice as large as those of the Communist countries. This is fairly clearly indicated by the crude steel figures, which point to a capacity in the non-Communist group which was about 2.3 times that of the Communist and a primary energy consumption of 1.84 times. If it were possible to allow for the quality of the finished steel represented by the crude, for the efficiency factor in primary energy consumption, and for the backwardness of the consumer goods industries in most Communist countries, the comparison would be even more favourable to the non-Communist. It is enough

THE ECONOMIES OF THE WORLD

Country or Region	Population in 1962 Millions	Crude Steel Output in 1962		Primary Energy Consumption in 1961[h]		Average Yearly Grain[1] Output in 1960/62	
		Million metric tons	Kgms. per head	Million metric tons	Kgms. per head	Million metric tons	Kgms. per head
Communist							
USSR	221	76.30	345	637	2,921	139.8	627
Eastern Europe and Yugoslavia	119	25.74	216	332	2,815	57.3	482
China	706	7.00	10⎫			180.0	255
N. Korea and			⎬	407	528		
N. Vietnam ..	28	1.05	37⎭			9.8	351
Total ..	1,074	110.09	103	1,376	1,290	386.9	360
English Speaking W. European and Allied[a]							
USA	187	89.20[e]	477	1,478	8.042	171.7	918
UK	53	20.82[f]	393	261	4,925	9.4	179
W. Germany ..	57	32.56[g]	571	204	3,626	12.9	226
France ..	47	17.24	367	116	2,514	21.4	453
Japan ..	95	27.61	291	122	1,298	19.9	209
Others	189	44.18	234	409	2,197	72.5	384
Total ..	628	231.61	369	2,590	4,184	307.8	490
Africa, Asia and Latin America[b]							
Latin America[c]	223	5.00	22	148	677	44.7	201
Africa	269	2.87	11	69	264	39.3	146
South Africa ..	16	2.63	164	43	2,414	5.9	372
Other Africa ..	253	0.24	1	26	106	33.4	132
Free Asia[d] ..	955	5.60	5	146	163	183.8	192
Total ..	1,447	13.47	9	363	264	267.8	185

[a] Including all non-Communist countries of Europe, but not their non-European territories; including Canada, Australia and New Zealand.

[b] Excluding Japan, but including all Colonial territories.

[c] Including Carribean islands.

[d] Including Pacific islands not included elsewhere.

[e] Output in 1955 was 106.17 million tons.

[f] Output in 1960 was 24.69 million tons.

[g] Output in 1960 was 34.1 million tons.

[h] Hard coal, brown coal, crude oil, natural gas and hydroelectricity, expressed in terms of hard coal equivalent.

[1] Wheat, rye, barley, oats, maize, millet, sorghum and rice.

Sources: United Nations Population and Vital Statistics Report.
United Nations Statistical Yearbook.
United Nations Monthly Bulletin of Statistics.
FAO Production Yearbook.

for our purposes, however, to show that for sheer size, the non-Communist industries as a whole continue to dwarf completely those of the Communist.

As one of the chief means of improving general standards of living, industrialization is essential. To some extent, therefore, the figures of crude steel output and primary energy consumption per head of population are indicators of living standards. It must, however, be borne in mind that the excessive preoccupation of the Communist countries with steel and heavy industrial production for their own sakes, and with armament production, causes these figures to exaggerate considerably the extent to which their living standards are catching up with those of the developed countries of the non-Communist world. Despite this preoccupation, the people of the Communist world had little more than a quarter of the steel capacity and well under a third of the primary energy consumption per person of the English-speaking peoples, Western Europeans and Japanese. This suggests that, to achieve the moderate living standards of the latter, the Communist world would require at the very least industries between three and four times their present size. (The word 'moderate' is used advisedly, for although the USA and Canada enjoy the highest material living standards in the world, these are counter-balanced by those of the remaining members of the non-Communist group, which includes a number of countries whose standards are moderate and others where they can only be described as poor. Nor should it be overlooked that the USA and Canada have enough poor people to make an increase in the average standard there also desirable.)

A rough indication of relative living standards is also provided by the grain output figures. It is hardly surprising that the total grain output of the Communist world is one-third greater than that of the English-speaking countries, Western Europe and Japan, since it has many more people to feed and since far the largest occupation of its people is agriculture. Even so, the amount of grain output per head of population is almost 30 per cent less in the Communist than in the non-Communist group. This does not, however, represent the full extent of the difference in feeding standards, because the better the diet the smaller the amount of bread and potatoes consumed and the greater the consumption of meat, dairy produce, green vegetables and fruit. As will be shown in more detail later in the case of the USSR, the agriculture of the whole Communist bloc is most inefficient and a drag on living standards and economic progress as a whole.

B

The economic backwardness of the Communist world is made to look as serious as it does largely because of China. She accounts for two-thirds of the population, has only been Communist for some fourteen years and is still an under-developed country. In fairness, therefore, comparison should also be made between the USSR and Communist Eastern Europe on the one hand and the USA and Western Europe on the other. Between the USA, which Khrushchev himself chooses as the yardstick, and the USSR, the comparison is wholly favourable to the former. In 1962 American steel capacity was about 60 per cent greater than Soviet capacity and current output of crude steel 16 per cent greater, giving an output per head of population which, in crude tonnage, was nearly 38 per cent greater. This comparison is, however, unduly favourable to the USSR, since it ignores the quality factor, which would be indicated to some extent at least if the comparison were of finished steel consumption by product. A truer reflection of the development of the two economies is probably provided by the figures of primary energy consumption. In 1961, the USA consumed 2.32 times more than the Soviet Union and 2.75 times more per head of population.

Estimates of the true relative levels of Soviet and of American industrial output as a whole, vary. When it is attempted to value industrial production and to apply a suitable exchange rate, the USSR itself considers that its output was already 65 per cent of the American in 1963, but American economists say that it was under 50 per cent. Taken together, the crude steel output and the primary energy consumption figures may perhaps be considered to point to Soviet industrial output of between 40 and 50 per cent of the American in 1960. For the USSR, with a population over 17 per cent greater than the USA, to have an industry only half the size of America is a far cry from Khrushchev's claim that, by 1970, Soviet industry will produce more per head of population than the USA.

The figures of American and Soviet grain production do not reveal the full extent of the superiority of American agriculture. Thus, although the average grain harvest of the USA is 23 per cent greater than that of the USSR and the output per head of population is 46 per cent greater, indicating a much greater American consumption of meat and dairy products, the figures tell nothing about the size of the respective agricultural labour forces. Thus, in the USSR, some 38 million people were employed in agriculture in the late 1950's, compared with 7 million in the USA. The average American agricultural worker is about eight times as productive as the average Soviet agricultural worker.

The figures also point to the greater degree of industrialization of such Western European countries as Britain, West Germany, and France. The total steel output of the present members of the European Economic Community—nearly 73 million tons—approaches that of the USSR, with West Germany at present producing more steel per head of population than the USA. If Britain had joined the European Economic Community, the group could have claimed almost as great an industrial capacity as that of the USSR and her satellites combined, yet its population would have been about a third less.

Latin America, Africa and Free Asia, other than Japan, contain many races and countries with a few much better off and much, better organized than the rest. Indeed, it may seem unrealistic to lump the relative prosperity of South Africa, for example, with the poverty of the rest of Africa to make the latter appear a shade less poor than it really is. But to single out all the individual political units of the three continents would be tedious and confusing. Only the broadest generalizations can be made, but so great is the contrast between the figures for these continents and those of the more developed countries that the breadth of the generalizations hardly matters. We are not now concerned so much with absolute economic power as with the degree of under-development, so we shall look straight away at figures of output and consumption per head of population. For convenience, these are presented as percentages of those for the English-speaking countries, Western Europe and Japan. The figures for the Communist world are also taken into consideration.

CRUDE STEEL OUTPUT, PRIMARY ENERGY CONSUMPTION
AND GRAIN OUTPUT PER HEAD OF POPULATION EXPRESSED
AS PERCENTAGES OF THOSE OF THE ENGLISH SPEAKING
PEOPLES, WESTERN EUROPE AND JAPAN

	Population (Million)	Crude Steel Output	Primary Energy Consumption	Grain Output
English Speaking, W. Europeans and Japan	628	100.0	100.0	100.0
Latin America	223	5.9	16.2	41
Free Asia	955	1.3	3.8	39
South Africa	16	44	58	75
Rest of Africa	253	0.3	2.6	27
China	706	2.7	13	51
USSR, Eastern Europe and Yugoslavia	340	81	68	120

The difference between the average levels of industrialization of Latin America, Free Asia and Africa and the rest of the world, other than China, is enormous. As a whole, Free Asia and Africa are virtually unindustrialized. Latin America is still at about the same industrial level as China despite the ambitious industrialization programmes of the latter, but both are hopelessly behind the 'capitalist' countries and the USSR and Eastern Europe.

As might be expected, grain output per head in the three great under-developed continents is far below that of the rest of the world, but the differences are much smaller than in the case of industry. These statistics, inadequate though they are, speak of mass hardship and privation, tempered or aggravated in varying degree by warm climates. It is necessary only to consider the short expectation of life in the under-developed regions compared with the industrialized countries, Communist or non-Communist, to obtain some idea of the extent of human suffering endured by the former. Although some of the vital statistics are scanty and of varying dates, they are adequate to illustrate this point.

United Nations statistics show that whereas in the industrialized countries, whether Communist or not, the expectation of life at birth for a male is now about 65 years, the average expectation in South America is, on the latest data available (pre-1952), somewhat under 50 years. In Continental Asia in the 1950s it was also below 50 years. In India, for example, it was just over 45 years in 1957–58. Among African negroes the expectation is under 40 years, having been as low as 30.5 years in rural Guinea as recently as 1954–55 and 35 years (for males and females together) in the Ivory Coast in 1956–58. However, in South Africa and Southern Rhodesia the expectation of life for the native population is considerably higher: 45 years in South Africa in 1950–52; 48 years in Southern Rhodesia in 1953–55.

To people in countries where the average expectation of life at birth is now between 65 and 70 years, the figures for Latin America, Africa and Asia are appalling. Yet, as recently as 1838–54 the average expectation of life in England and Wales was as little as 39.91 years.[1] Generalizations are dangerous, but few will seriously disagree that a situation in which the average expectation of life is under 50 years is one of widespread human suffering, or that the most important way so far discovered by man to eliminate this suffering has involved a revolution in agricultural techniques and industrialization. Misery acute enough to cut twenty to forty years off man's span has only recently been banished from the main

[1] A. M. Carr-Saunders, *World Population*.

industrial countries, but it still afflicts at least 45 per cent of the world's population and, were the facts in China known, possibly as many as 68 per cent.

Consideration of the economic statistics for the three great world groups shows that there is much less in Khrushchev's boasts of Communist strength than he would have us believe. In terms of total national production, the economy of the USA is much stronger than the Soviet, and perhaps even stronger than the whole Communist world combined. The industrial output of the European Economic Community is close to that of the Soviet. Where output per head of population is concerned, the US economy is incomparably superior to that of the USSR; the European Economic Community and Britain are also far ahead. The backwardness of the Soviet and East European economies is nothing to that of China or of Latin America, Continental Asia and Africa, where there is widespread human misery.

Although Communist leaders generally admit that their economies are still not as powerful as some in the West, it is always asserted that this is a temporary phenomenon, and that in a short time even the American giant will be outpaced by the Soviet Union. These forecasts are examined more carefully and their probability is given some preliminary consideration in the next chapter.

CHAPTER III

The Production Race

Though the Soviet economy in terms of absolute magnitude is still dwarfed by that of the United States it is expanding fast; faster, in fact, than its great western rival. Will it ever catch up, and, if so, when? As far as the Soviet leaders are concerned, the answer was given at the 22nd Party Congress in October, 1961. The new Party Programme, which outlines the country's economic tasks for the next twenty years, states that by 1970 the USSR will have surpassed the US level of industrial production and will have overtaken the USA in production per head of the main types of agricultural produce. Khrushchev in his speech on the second day of the congress went further. He boasted that by 1970, the USSR would be the first industrial power in the world, and would achieve superiority to the USA not only in overall industrial output, but also in the industrial output per head of population. He added that, by the same date, the USSR would have exceeded the USA's present output of agricultural products per head by one and a half times.

These forecasts are a vital feature of the Soviet twenty-year programme and it is easy to see why. The prospect of out-producing the richest and most powerful representative of capitalism with all the political, economic and strategic implications that that carries has a compelling attraction. It is claimed that the economic defeat of the United States would be the final proof of the superiority of Communism, and that this lesson would not be lost on the under-developed countries. Naturally, it is also intended to act as an incentive for the Soviet people themselves. Dry statistics look very different when seen in terms of a race with an affluent America, with the highest standard of living in the world as first prize. Finally, of course, the creation of such a mighty economy would widen the scope for manoeuvres in trade and aid and vastly increase the country's military potential.

How seriously are we to take Soviet forecasts? To delete the propaganda element and get down to hard facts presents difficulties. As indicated in Chapter II, it is hard enough to compare any two countries, but there are special hazards when it comes to the Soviet Union and the United States. Not only are their economies disparate but the amount of Soviet information is unusually meagre. Furthermore, Soviet propagandists have such a strong compulsion to prove that the USA is being overhauled that the figures they use are sometimes exaggerated and often misleading. To determine a date at which Soviet industrial output might conceivably draw level with that of the USA the present relative position, and the respective future growth rates have to be taken into account. Not surprisingly these are disputed. In the first place, it is almost impossible to get a meaningful estimate of the present ratio between the two industrial levels because of the complexity and infinite variety of production. Motor cars cannot be added to bread, for example, Nor are two Volga cars equivalent to one Chevrolet and one Cadillac. The only method which approaches a satisfactory solution to such problems is to use money valuations. This, provided proper allowance is made for changes in general price levels, will enable an individual country to compare its total output fairly satisfactorily in any given year with that in other years. It will also permit reasonable international comparisons between countries having similar price and currency systems and free exchange rates. But it is impossible to make satisfactory comparisons between such countries and those like the USSR where prices and exchange rates are fixed by the government and the quality of products in relation to the price cannot be properly assessed by outsiders. Various economists have tried to rework the Soviet production figures in western terms, but the comparisons thus made with the USA vary considerably. Even then, the final answers leave out such important considerations as the quality and range of goods and existing inventories. Suffice it to say that, as noted in the previous chapter, the USSR claims that it had already reached 65 per cent of US industrial level by 1963, while most western estimates put the figure at under 50 per cent.

The Soviet forecast also assumes that over the next decade the average annual rates of growth will be 9.6 per cent for the USSR and little more than 2.5 per cent for the USA. Ignoring the fact that the Soviet figure applies to *gross* industrial output, and that for the USA to net output[1] there is nothing to indicate that these rates will bear

[1] The Soviet gross output figure includes a certain amount of double-counting of intermediate products, whereas the US figure is a conventional 'value-added'

any relation to reality. Many western observers feel that as the Soviet economy expands it will become increasingly difficult to maintain a constant increment of around 10 per cent a year. Already, in 1963, the Soviet claim for gross industrial output has fallen to 8.5 per cent, and the plans for 1964 and 1965 foresee no immediate acceleration. The annual percentage rate of growth of industry usually tends to be much faster in the early years than when the economy reaches maturity. There are a number of reasons for this: the much greater availability of fresh labour supplies for industry in the early growth stages than later, when the heavy reserves attached to agriculture have been absorbed by industry as a result both of the improvement of labour saving agricultural techniques and the attraction to the countryman of life in the industrial areas; the exhaustion of the richest and more accessible mineral deposits; the growth of inflexibility due to such factors as the increased power of trade unions and social legislation; and the increasing emphasis on replacement of existing industrial capacity rather than on the further extension of new capacity. The rapid industrial growth rates now being experienced by certain Communist countries were experienced by Britain in the late eighteenth and early nineteenth centuries and by western Europe and the USA in the late nineteenth and early twentieth centuries. They are also characteristic in countries recovering from the severe setback of a modern war. Rapid growth is particularly easy when there is a large leeway to make up. Also, when it becomes desirable or necessary (as has happened in recent years) to allocate a larger share of total resources to defence and space, housing, consumer services, agriculture and transport, rather than to direct productive investment in industry, the rate of growth of industry will diminish.

In fact, when looked at more carefully, Khrushchev's confident prediction is reduced to a conflicting and confusing range of possibilities. His bold statements should more properly be regarded as exhortations rather than nearly accomplished facts. If it is assumed that the western estimate of the 1963 ratio of the two industries (no more than 50 : 100) is more realistic, which it certainly is, and that Soviet industry will grow at some 8 per cent a year and the US at 3 per cent (1951–62 was 3.9 per cent), then the USSR would still be about 20 per cent behind by 1970, and as much as 30 per cent behind on a per caput basis.

calculation. Most western experts, and now even some Soviet commentators, consider that the index of gross industrial output is inflated, and the rate of growth expressed in net terms would be much slower. For details see Appendix I.

Even when comparisons are made using specific commodities there are pitfalls; these are often deliberately overlooked by Soviet propagandists. There are, for instance, differences in measurement. US coal production is measured after cleaning and sorting; Soviet output is not. Moreover the calorific value of much of Soviet coal is lower than the US product, so figures quoted in millions of tons give a deceptive picture. In international comparisons it is always difficult to make allowances for quality and variety of output. Soviet comparisons of commodity output invariably contrast relative production levels, ignoring the fact that in the USA there is often a large gap, both between production and consumption, and between production and capacity. In 1960, the relative level of oil production was USSR 43, USA 100; but if the same calculation is done on the basis of consumption (making allowance for imports and exports) the ratio becomes USSR 26, USA 100. Similarly, the output of crude steel in the USSR was 72 per cent of the US level of 1960, but the ratio only about 45 per cent in terms of production capacities.

Finally, comparisons between the two countries often fail to take account of different or changing patterns of consumption. The USSR already claims to have passed the USA in the output of woollen textiles, but US wool production is declining because of the greater use of synthetic fibres. The lack of information on future trends in US commodity production over the next decade makes comparison with the figures given by Khrushchev for the Soviet Union impossible. One exception is electric power output for which projections have been made by the Federal Power Commission. Using these, it can be estimated that by 1970 the USSR will still be generating only about two-thirds of US electric power output. The USSR will almost certainly exceed the present output of steel in the USA by 1970, but will still be at least ten years behind reckoning in steel melting capacity and even further behind in terms of capacity per head of population. Oil production may pass the present US level, but consumption will still be below it.

In agriculture, the problem is rather different. As a major pre-occupation of the US Government is the need to reduce over-production in agriculture, it is surely a race with one self-appointed runner. Almost half the Soviet working population, compared with some 10 per cent in America, produces no more than about 60 per cent of US output for a population 20 per cent larger. This shows itself in the lack of protein and variety in an only just adequate diet stuffed with calories from bread and potatoes. The new Soviet economic programme forecasts that during the next decade the

USSR will overtake the USA in production per head of the main types of agricultural produce. The Soviet Union is already ahead as regards wheat, potatoes, flax, sugar beet and wool. The following table gives data for some other commodities:

OUTPUT PER HEAD OF AGRICULTURAL PRODUCE
(kilogrammes)

	USA		USSR				
	1960	1961	1960	1962	1963	1970 Plan	1980 Plan
Grain	1070	895	623	670	572	945–1065	1042–1115
Meat	95	99	40	43	46	82.0–102.5	108–115
Milk	317	310	288	290	273	472–554	612–647
Butter	3.8	3.8	4.0	4.3	3.9	5.0*	
Eggs	369	346	127	136	129	272	404

* 1965.

If it is assumed that the American production per head will change little in the next ten years, then the figures show that, according to the plan, the US level will be reached for meat and milk by 1970, but for grain and eggs at a much later date. As there is little likelihood of this plan being fulfilled, the claims cannot be taken too seriously. The American citizen will without doubt still be eating more meat, eggs, vegetables and fruit in 1970 and probably even in 1980 than his Soviet counterpart. During the past four years (1959–63), agricultural production in the USSR has actually declined and the diet of the bulk of the population must have deteriorated. As a consequence the 1970 plans for agriculture have already been slightly modified.

An interesting sidelight on these rather spurious production competitions is provided by the fate of an earlier challenge. In 1957 Khrushchev caught the world's attention by announcing that the USSR would 'catch up with the USA in the production per head of population of milk and butter by 1958 and meat by 1960 or 1961.' This was so obviously impossible (except for butter which could be promoted at the expense of milk or cheese) that even Khrushchev's economists told him so. By the end of 1959 the butter claim was, slightly belatedly, made good, though no mention was made of the relatively larger amounts of margarine consumed as a matter of preference in the USA. The boasts about meat and milk have not yet been honoured, and it will be a long time before they are.

There is one final consideration. Disregarding the statistical snags, it can be argued that it is erroneous to compare the two economies because of their different pattern, purpose and degree of maturity. By the same argument it can be said that Khrushchev's slogan, 'catch up with the USA,' is almost meaningless except in its propaganda context. For one thing, comparisons of growth rates and relative ratios are likely to give an inaccurate picture of the real situation facing the consumer. Important questions of quality have to be disregarded as well as the variety and range of products. The efficiency of the distribution system makes for considerable qualitative differences as does the general availability of services. Comparisons also mask the purpose and direction of an economy. In the USA the economy is primarily orientated to the satisfaction of the domestic consumer, while in the Soviet Union the main aim is the establishment of a strong industrial base, often at the expense of consumer demands.

What is fairly clear is that at present the US economy on any calculation is far ahead of the Soviet, but that until recently Soviet growth rates have been generally faster than the American. In 1962 and 1963 the growth of the Soviet economy slowed significantly, largely as a result of the failures in agriculture, with increases in GNP of some 5 per cent and 3 per cent, compared with gains by the USA of 6 per cent and 4 per cent. If the Soviet rate of growth were to resume even a slight lead over the American then, mathematically speaking, a cross over point would be reached some time. This will be long after 1970. It is worth emphasising again that rapid growth rates are not the prerogative of Communist economies, and stagnation the inescapable consequence of a capitalist system. Between 1953 and 1960, the industrial output of Japan increased more than two and a half times, while all the Soviet official index for the same period can claim is a doubling of production. Similarly, steel output has been rising considerably faster in the countries of the European Economic Community in the last decade than in the USSR.

The Soviet Union has not been the only Communist country to single out some western rival for competition: China and East Germany have also indulged in this pursuit. The former announced about four years ago that she would, by 1970, outstrip Britain in the output of major industrial products. This aim, which was not expressed in terms of output per head, was about as vague as Khrushchev's plan for pushing Soviet agricultural production up to the American level, and since the British population is about one-fourteenth of the Chinese, is plainly ridiculous. Nonetheless, it probably served some purpose for internal propaganda. There was more point in East Germany's announced intention at roughly the same time to give the population a higher consumption per head of foodstuffs and of the most important industrial goods than West Germany by the end of 1961. This was to be with Soviet backing and had its major object the elimination of unfavourable comparisons of East German living conditions with those of the Federal Republic by a population which was only too ready to flee across the frontier. The figures forecast for 1961 in this competiton did not stand up to much examination; they concerned private cars, refrigerators, roasted coffee and cocoa products, shoes, textiles and foodstuffs.

In the meantime, the Chinese economy has run into serious difficulties, brought about by the excesses of an over-rapid industrialization programme, gross mismanagement of agriculture, which has been the victim of political experimentation, and a series of natural disasters resulting in bad harvests. Currently, the 'great leap forward' in industry and the socialization of agriculture have been shelved. For the time being, at least, the emphasis is on retrenchment and on the rescuing of agriculture from its misfortunes at the expense of the industrial programme, so it is unlikely that much more will be heard for some time of overtaking British industry. The East German economy has also run into serious difficulties for broadly similar reasons. The pace of industrialization has proved much too fast for her limited resources and the over-zealous collectivization of agriculture in 1960 was disastrous for food production. Instead of providing the population with a higher standard of living than that of the Federal Republic, the East German authorities merely caused so great an upsurge in the flow of refugees from a life that had become intolerable that they were forced to erect a containing wall between East and West Berlin in August, 1961. How much the complete failure of this particular competition contributed to the international crisis over Berlin is a matter for speculation.

CHAPTER IV

Expenditure on Defence and Aid to
the Uncommitted Countries

On its own admission the Soviet Union continues to spend large sums on its armed forces both directly in the form of arms production and maintenance of service personnel and indirectly in the form of military research and development. Closely allied to this are the space and atomic energy programmes. Despite Khrushchev's protestations of peaceful intentions, the military significance of these latter is enormous, as also is their cost. One of the main criticisms of Stalin was that he gave so much attention to military strength that he brought the Soviet economy to the brink of disaster and made a mockery of the workers' paradise, the creation of which was claimed to be one of Communism's chief aims. How great is the continuing burden of these non-economic activities, so essential perhaps in Communist eyes, to the security of the Communist system and to its prestige in the outside world, but so inhibiting to the development of its material welfare?

Much has been heard in recent years about the growing volume of material aid provided by the Soviet Union and other Communist Powers to African, Asian and Latin American countries. This has been largely in the form of capital equipment and technical advice and, in many cases, has included important consignments of armaments. From some of the publicity given to these transactions it might be inferred that the Communist world was in danger of slowing the development of its own economies to secure influence in the uncommitted countries. Clearly, if this aid were entirely or mainly unrequited and on a large scale, it could have such an effect, so this problem, too, must be examined.

Defence and Space
The effort that goes into the defence and associated space pro-

gramme must be looked at qualitatively as well as quantitatively. In the centrally-planned economies of the Communist countries, all activity is governed by a strict order of preference. In the case of the Soviet Union, defence comes first, in spite of the official interest shown in such civil programmes as housing, argiculture, consumer goods and the like. This does not mean that more is devoted to defence than to everything else, but that it absorbs the best human and material resources and that in the event of a conflict between it and a civil programme, defence considerations will usually prevail.

Military research and development absorb the best scientific brains while defence industries take the cream of technicians, the most sophisticated equipment, and the pick of raw materials. The results of this system are obvious. For example, simultaneously with the launching of manned space craft and the explosion of 50 megaton nuclear weapons, millions of pairs of shoes, too shoddy and old fashioned even for Soviet tastes, pile up unwanted in the shops. A recent article about the shortage of furniture in Kuybyshev oblast admitted that in 1961, 45 per cent of all furniture produced in the area was condemned and forbidden issue at factory level, while a further 47 per cent was rejected by retail trade organizations. These are only two instances of what is going on throughout the consumer sector of the Soviet economy. The production of nuclear submarines is not subject to the same wastage rates. The primary goal for many years has been to match or exceed the United States in military power, and more recently in astronautics, and attention has been centred on developing the economic base for military production rather than on making consumer items more abundant. What kind of real sacrifice has this been for the economy? Funds and resources poured into defence activities virtually have to be written off: military end items are soon obsolete, and the soldier is economically non-productive. The exceptions are where defence and allied research programmes yield, as by-products, inventions or techniques capable of civil application. But the valuable resources devoted to developing and producing the intricate mechanisms and electronic devices for missile and space projects are denied to those automation schemes which are so vital to the rapid achievement of the level of industrial productivity implicit in the aim of catching up the USA in the next decade. When we try to discover how much, quantitatively, the Soviet defence and space effort impinges on the economy, we can only use approximations, because the USSR is abnormally secretive about these matters.

The only two published figures which have any relevance at all are the annual budget allocations for 'Defence' and 'Science'. No details are published about the amounts spent under these two main categories whereas, in the USA, many pages in the annual budget are given about each of them. In Britain, too, a great deal is given, running into several volumes. Many western students have dismissed these scanty Soviet figures as mere propaganda, designed to impress the world with the USSR's peaceful pre-occupations, but this conclusion does not bear close examination. For example, the budgetary allocation to defence is substantial. Moreover, when it is considered in the light of what it is said by Soviet financial text books to cover and, by implication, what it does not cover, it makes sense. To demonstrate this is a somewhat complicated matter requiring the study of a good deal of varied data bearing on Soviet defence activity. It is best treated in a self-contained appendix. From such a study it emerges that Soviet defence expenditure, as stated in the budget, mostly consists of what is spent directly on equipping and maintaining the armed forces. Little would appear to be allocated under this heading to research and development. The amounts officially stated to have been budgeted are ample for forces as large as those claimed by Khrushchev to have existed at various specified times. The forces could have been provided with a supply first of conventional weapons and latterly a growing proportion of unconventional weapons so as to make them roughly as strong as reasonable people in the west consider them to be.

Such are the size and rate of growth of the 'Science' Vote and the similarity of its growth to that of American expenditure on military research and development that it is inconceivable that the greater part of it is not used for this purpose. But there are strong reasons for believing that expenditure on the Soviet nuclear energy programme may not be included in the 'Defence' or 'Science' Votes at all: it is more likely to be covered by the great 'National Economy' Vote under the sub-heading (never disclosed) of medium machine building. This is unsatisfactory for the western student but, as can be seen from the collateral evidence given in Appendix II, it does not entirely preclude reasonable if somewhat rough estimates, which are all that are necessary for our present purposes. One of the main considerations here is that since the USSR is striving to compete with the USA in all aspects of military, space, and nuclear energy research and development and has scored considerable successes in these spheres, the total Soviet outlay must be large. The corresponding American outlay is known and provides valuable guidance to the order of magnitude of the Soviet outlay.

The latest year for which information permits a reasonably satisfactory analysis of defence spending in both countries was 1960. This is the most recent year for which official Soviet data about both defence expenditure and armed forces strengths are available. Taking the official figures of Soviet 'direct' defence expenditure in 1960 of 9.3 thousand million roubles[1] at a rouble/dollar ratio suggested by the Joint Economic Committee of the US Congress, it must have been roughly equivalent to $23.25 thousand million. The corresponding US expenditure in that year was $37.4 thousand million, hence the Soviet expenditure was roughly 62 per cent of the American. Such is the emphasis laid on military, space and atomic energy research and development by the USSR that it would be reasonable to assume that their combined outlay may have been equivalent to some 80 per cent of the American. This means that the total direct and indirect defence and space efforts of the USSR would, in 1960, have absorbed approximately two-thirds of the money spent on the corresponding programmes by the USA. This may seem modest, but it implies Soviet programmes about five times as great as those of Britain, although the Soviet national income was less than three times that of Britain and the Soviet population was over four times as great — a heavy burden for a poor country. It is this kind of comparison which makes it hard to accept the view that, apart from the atomic energy programme, the USSR has been secretly spending large sums on defence other than under the announced 'Defence' and 'Science' Votes.

A rough indication of the total burdens of direct and indirect defence and atomic energy outlays borne by the economies of the USA and the USSR in 1960 is shown below in terms of US dollars.

US AND SOVIET DEFENCE BURDEN IN 1960

	USA	USSR
Population (millions)	177	216
Gross National Product $000,000,000	500*	235*
Income per head (dollars)	2,825	1,088
Total Defence, Space and Atomic Energy Outlay $000,000,000	46.1	30
Defence Expenditure per head (dollars)	260	139
Defence Effort as a per cent of Gross National Product	9.2	12.8

* Based on the US Congress Joint Economic Committee's report 'Dimensions of Soviet Economic Power'.

[1] The values given in this book are in terms of the new rouble, introduced in January 1961. One new rouble is worth ten pre-1961 roubles.

These figures show that, as far as can be judged, the Soviet Gross National Product was about 53 per cent less than that of the USA, although the Soviet population was about 22 per cent larger. Thus, the Soviet income per head was a little under 40 per cent of the American. About 9 per cent of the average US income was absorbed by defence, space and the atomic energy programme and 12.8 per cent of the Soviet. So great is the American compared with the Soviet average income per head that if the USA had trebled the 1960 defence and atomic energy outlay, the amount per head remaining for other purposes would still have been about double that available for non-defence purposes in the USSR.

It is still too early to reach any firm conclusions about the burden of Soviet defence expenditure after 1960. Since then, budgetary allocations to defence have risen dramatically. For instance, taken on its face value, the 'direct' outlay proposed for 1963 was, at 13,900 million roubles, almost 50 per cent higher than it was in 1960 and would have been equivalent to about 80 per cent of the direct defence expenditure of the USA. If, however, as is suspected, it was deliberately inflated for political reasons by the transfer to it of items not previously classified as defence, the quoted percentage is too high. The most likely items to have been transferred are military stockpiling and defence investment. To judge from the growth of the 'Science' vote, the USSR, like the USA, may in 1963 have been spending a little over 40 per cent more on defence research and development and the space programmes than she was in 1960, hence there may have been no reduction of the American lead in these departments as a whole during the last three years. Despite the rapid growth of Soviet direct and indirect defence expenditure in recent years, it continues to be appreciably smaller than that of the USA.

Having been caught unawares by the Korean War in 1950 and having subsequently been goaded by the USSR's provocative achievements with inter-continental ballistic missiles and space vehicles, and having very nearly been caught in Cuba, the USA is leaving nothing to chance, particularly as she has the capacity to do so without unduly burdening her population. The published statistics of the USSR and the USA shown in Table 1 of Appendix II support this conclusion. Thus, American service strengths and defence expenditure were drastically cut after the Second World War, whereas those of the USSR remained exceptionally high. It was Soviet defence expenditure which first began to rise rapidly again in the late 1940s. If Soviet defence and allied expenditure is now partly to blame for its serious economic problems it has nobody to blame but itself for entering into competi-

C

tion in these spheres with a country so economically powerful as the USA.

Aid to the Uncommitted Countries

Unlike the figures of defence expenditure, those of bloc economic aid to the developing countries can be fairly reasonably estimated from official broadcasts and newspapers both of the countries granting such aid and of those receiving it. Between 1954 and 1963, the USSR entered into agreements with nearly thirty countries, committing itself to credits worth some $3,600 millions. During the same period, the East European countries entered into agreements with some thirty countries (most of them the same as those covered by the USSR) but the total value promised was probably not more than $1,300 millions. Chinese agreements, which were not undertaken before 1956, have been with fifteen countries by the end of 1963, and were rather more than $500 millions.

For various reasons, there is a considerable time lag between the granting of a development credit and its implementation. Thus, although the USSR granted credits in 1960 of over $800 millions, yearly drawings do not appear to have gone much above $300 millions. For Eastern Europe, drawings have been between $60 and $100 million a year and for China under $15 million a year. Such amounts are not a strain on the Communist economies. If drawings on the USSR had been as much as $200 millions in 1960, these would have accounted for no more than 0.1 per cent of national income and 0.7 per cent of direct and indirect defence expenditure combined. Much the same is true of Eastern Europe and China. Moreover, since the national incomes of the USSR and its satellites have grown since 1960, it is unlikely that the relative 'burden' of these development credits is any greater today than it was two or three years ago. In any case, most of the aid takes the form of medium-term credits, albeit at the low interest rates charged within the Communist economies for their own purposes, and redeemable largely in the products, mainly foodstuffs and raw materials, of the recipient countries. It is debatable, therefore, whether the development credits constitute any burden to the Communist economies.

Fairly significant amounts of military equipment have been delivered to various countries in Asia, Africa and the Middle East and to Cuba, but the total value is not known. This lack of precise data does not pose a serious problem. Most of the armaments delivered, although important to the recipients are, from the Soviet standpoint, obsolescent. They will, therefore, have been paid for out of past defence budgets and, even if the value were known, it would be double counting to add it to the current burden of Soviet defence expenditure. The deliveries are seldom free of charge and could even be regarded as materially advantageous to the bloc, quite apart from the political advantages which are their main motive.

Figures of the long-term aid granted to developing countries by the NATO powers and Japan are now published by the Organization for Economic Co-operation and Development (OECD) in Paris. They show how small Communist aid has been so far, not only in relation to national income but to what is being granted by the main non-Communist countries. In 1962, for example, the total flow of financial resources to developing countries was worth $8,400 million, of which $5,957 million consisted of 'official grants and grant-like contributions'. The latter figure is nearly ten times as much as was promised by the bloc in 1962 and about twenty times as much as was actually transferred. No comparison can be made between the amounts of military aid granted by the two groups.

Large though the aid granted by the NATO and Japanese governments is compared with that granted by the Communist Powers it is completely dwarfed when compared with national income and to defence expenditure. In the case of the USA, the most generous of all the western countries, such official aid amounted to only 0.7 per cent of national income in 1960 and 6.2 per cent of direct and indirect defence expenditure. These are better figures than the 0.1 per cent and 0.7 per cent, respectively, of national income and defence expenditure of the USSR, but it is clear that both powers devote more resources in the armaments race than to foreign aid programmes. Broadly the same is true of other industrial countries, Communist and non-Communist alike. In no case can the volume of aid to the developing countries be seriously compared with defence expenditure. The problem of foreign aid are discussed in greater detail in Chapter XI.

CHAPTER V

Inherent Advantages and Disadvantages
of the Communist Economies

In looking at the problem of the Communist economic potential, the diversion of resources into the arms and space race, is a limiting factor on growth. This is a burden voluntarily assumed by the governments concerned although, given the nature of international society, it would be unrealistic to think they had much choice. It would be unrealistic, too, to ignore certain disadvantages of geography, geology and climate which have been important among the reasons why the economies of the USSR, Eastern and Central Europe and China were later in their expansion than Western Europe and the USA. Moreover, because they are permanent, these disadvantages still have to be contended with.

The USSR has huge deposits of coal, oil and iron ore, which are the principal bulk resources for industrialization, as well as vast forests which can provide an almost unlimited supply of timber both for industry and construction and for fuel, but its raw materials are situated far apart. Moreover, though it has many great rivers, they mostly flow in the wrong directions, i.e. into the Arctic Ocean, instead of linking coal with ore deposits. In any case, the prolonged winters freeze the rivers for many months at a time, severely damage the roads and make life difficult for the builders and maintainers of railways. Many of the richest resources are remote and in climatically inhospitable regions where few people would choose to live. In the rest of Eastern and Central Europe, mineral deposits essential to industry are few and far between. Even Polish coal is not particularly suitable for metallurgy, while the high quality coking coal of Moravia is limited in quantity; there is little indigenous iron ore. The natural conditions for cheap, bulk, water transport are poor though, like the climate, they are not so adverse as in the USSR.

China's natural disadvantages are every bit as great. She is fairly richly endowed with minerals, but they are widely scattered and, somewhat like the USSR, she has to contend with great distances along inland routes. Her worst problems, however, are caused by flooding —injurious to industry as well as to agriculture—and by her mountainous terrain, with 60 per cent of her area over 6,000 feet above sea level. In contrast the countries of Western Europe and North America enjoy natural resources conveniently close together or accessible by water and have, as a whole, a friendlier climate. All this makes for much lower production costs, which obviously affect living standards.

Though the Communist political and economic system is one geared for growth it acts, in many ways, as a brake upon itself. The various features of the planned economy of Communism—both those that provide its dynamism and those that create confusion, inefficiency and waste, will have to be examined.

Ever since the accession of Stalin, the overriding considerations in the Soviet Union have been the creation of an up-to-date defence capacity and the stimulation of the fastest possible economic growth. The latter has supported the former and has been very much a matter of concentrating on the promotion of basic and heavy industry rather than on the production of consumer goods. This has been a deliberate act of government economic policy implemented by means of centralised planning which attempts to control virtually the whole of economic life. The plan is the kernel. It states how much of almost every important product must be produced each month, quarter, year or period of years. Normally it is only the yearly, five-yearly or longer term production plans which are published. These are mostly for the country as a whole, but each region, works and other individual undertaking also has its plan. The growth-stimulating, the defence-supporting branches of the economy, such as metallurgy and engineering, are given the most ambitious production aims, and are helped to achieve them by various means, particularly in the allocation of investment funds and of equipment, materials and labour.

The State owns practically the whole of industry and the transport system, and controls all agricultural activity; two-thirds of total housing is publicly owned. This widespread State and public ownership naturally lends itself to central economic planning. It may be considered that it is the public ownership that is fundamental to socialism, but what gives the Communist economy its particular stamp is the planning, with its emphasis on stimulating production and productivity and on their corollary, the system of priorities and controlled prices. Western countries nowadays go in for varying amounts of public ownership of economic undertakings, but, except in wartime, they have never gone to the lengths in central economic planning that have been reached under Communism, particularly in the USSR. It is the Communist Party, ostensibly acting for the good of the whole community, that replaces the unseen hand of market forces which still plays so great a part in the operation of a non-Communist economy despite all the controls imposed in recent years. Communism claims that this is the only rational way of developing an economy—to control, not be controlled, even partially. Before the teachings of Keynes were absorbed by western policy makers, when economic growth was irregular and unemployment could be both frequent and prolonged, there was force in this argument. Moreover, in time of war, when the need to promote certain specific and relatively limited types of production has been paramount, non-Communist countries have not hesitated to resort to a system of deliberate production plans, priorities, rationing and controls both of supplies and prices.

When the Communists came to power in countries which, owing to the circumstances of geography, climate and history were economically backward compared with Western Europe and North America, it seemed logical to men like Stalin to use the methods of war economy to overcome this backwardness.

If, as it seems, it is a matter of growth for growth's sake, does not the centrally-planned, publicly-owned economy enjoy considerable advantages, particularly in investment, defence expenditure, and the control of social services and wages? In this age of costly capital equipment and complicated armaments requiring huge expenditure, the ability of the authorities to assemble the funds required by means of indirect taxation, without having to attract the investor or to face Press and parliamentary criticism, is of the first importance. The same applies to the allocation of investment and other State expenditure. The limits set are the availability of the resources. Theoretically there is little to prevent the realization of those productive projects that are the vital elements of rapid growth. Thirty years of sacrifice by the Soviet consumer have built a powerful economy; it is authoritarian central planning that has made this possible.

The USSR and most of its European satellites claim to be devoting between 25 and 30 per cent of their national products to investment and accumulation. In view of the high proportion also devoted to defence, particularly by the USSR, such an allocation for investment is remarkable, even allowing for the peculiarities of Communist statistics. The following table compares the ratio of Soviet investments to gross national product in 1955, suitably adjusted to render them comparable with those of the OEEC (or Marshall Plan) countries and the USA in the same year.

Country	Ratio of Investment to Gross National Product Per Cent
Britain	16.3
Belgium	25.0
Netherlands	24.6
W. Germany	25.4
France	18.5
Italy	19.0
Other OEEC Countries	17.5
All OEEC	19.8
USA	20.3
USSR	25.2

Based on Table 32 of 'Comparative National Products and Price Levels' by Milton Gilbert and Associates (OEEC, Paris) and 'Comparisons of the United States and Soviet Economies' (Joint Economic Committee of US Congress). All figures for 1955.

Even after readjustment, the ratio of investment in the USSR was well above the average for the USA and for the OEEC countries as a whole and very considerably above that of Britain.[1] Indeed, it is about the same as that of the most heavily investing OEEC countries— Belgium, the Netherlands and West Germany. This is all the more remarkable when it is considered how low is the average income per head in the USSR compared with those in Western Europe and the USA.

Comparison of the distribution of investments in Communist countries between the more immediately productive, or growth stimulating sectors, and other categories with the distribution in non-Communist countries, is more difficult. This is largely a matter of how investment statistics are classified. A full breakdown of State investments is provided by the USSR and there is apparently no attempt to conceal the tremendous emphasis on productive, as distinct from amenity, investments. The table overleaf shows the distribution in the USSR between 1952 and 1958. The most nearly

[1] There has since been a considerable increase in the British investment ratio, but it is still slightly under 20 per cent of gross national production and thus well below the Soviet ratio.

comparable figures for Britain have been taken from the Economic Survey for 1961.

The USSR is seen to have allocated 61.3 per cent of its investments to industry and agriculture—the most immediately productive categories—whereas Britain's allocation was only 31.3 per cent. These percentages exaggerate the greater Soviet emphasis on 'productive' investments, because British 'other investments' include such items as gas which the USSR classes with oil and therefore with industrial investments as a whole. Nevertheless, if allowance could be made for these cases, the USSR would still be devoting a far higher proportion of her investments to the direct stimulation of production than is Britain. It should also be noted that, although

PERCENTAGE DISTRIBUTION OF INVESTMENTS

Category	USSR 1952–1958	Category	UK 1956–1960
Industry	45.4	Mining and Manufacturing	27.6
Agriculture and Forestry..	15.9	Agriculture, Forestry and Fishing	3.7
Transport and Communications	9.6	Transport and Communications*	12.3
Housing and Communal Services	18.4	Dwellings	18.3
Other Investments† ..	10.7	Other Investments‡ ..	38.1
Total	**100.0**	**Total**	**100.0**

* Excluding road goods transport.
† Including electricity generation.
‡ Including electricity generation, road goods transport and public services.

housing has been vigorously promoted in the USSR for the greater part of the post-Stalin era, it received no larger a share of total investments than it did in Britain, where the need is much less urgent.

The advantages enjoyed by Communist Governments are again great where wages are concerned. Trade unions are controlled to an extent which would neither be attempted nor tolerated in democratic countries. It would be unrealistic to say that the workers in Communist economies are completely debarred from using the trade unions as a means of obtaining improvements in pay and working conditions, particularly in the USSR under Khrushchev, but the fact remains that the unions are the creatures of the regime and act as its agents in enforcing the prescribed wages and hours and in the promotion of increased productivity. Indeed, a trade union in a

Communist country is more analogous to the suspect company trade unions to be found in some non-Communist countries than to the typical British trade union with its complete independence of the employer. This means that there is little question of the workers using the strike threat and none at all of official strikes. Communist economies are, therefore, almost free of that major problem of the present British economy and potential problem of the other democratic countries—the inflationary spiral. However, a degree of semi-repressed inflation has been experienced in the Soviet Union in recent years. As a result of the failures in agriculture and an unexpectedly heavy influx of workers into the towns, the planned balance between private purchasing power and the supply of consumer goods and services has been upset and demand has been greater than the supply of saleable goods at the prices fixed by the State. Physical shortages, lengthening queues, steeply rising prices on the 'free' collective farm markets, and a large involuntary growth in savings deposits have resulted. There are no direct repercussions on the production process in the State sector or on international trade. But such a state of affairs does cause popular discontent and the effect of this on the incentive to work can be important.

Figures on wages and productivity in various countries published in *The Economist*[1] can be used in conjunction with official Soviet and United Nations figures to illustrate the advantage enjoyed by the Soviet Government in its control over labour. The wage-cost indices below have been derived by applying the productivity indices to the wage indices. In only three of the seven countries covered has there been a fall in the wage-cost indices—Italy, Japan and the USSR, all of

WAGE COSTS ROUND THE WORLD
1952=100

	Productivity Index		Nominal Wage Index		Wage-Cost Index	
	1959	*1962*	*1959*	*1962*	*1959*	*1962*
USA	112.1	119.3	131.6	148.1	117.3	124.1
UK	119.3	125.7	138.5	153.4	116.1	122.0
France ..	152.6	182.1	168.0	210.2	110.1	115.4
W. Germany	131.4	150.5	150.7	206.3	114.6	137.1
Italy ..	165.4	215.4	161.4	208.9	97.6	97.0
Japan ..	163.2	227.7	153.8	201.9	94.2	88.7
USSR	164	191	121*	140*	74	73

* Estimated.

[1] March 24, 1962, page 1141, for figures up to 1959. Those for 1962 are based on industrial employment, production and wage data in the United Nations' Monthly Bulletins of Statistics.

whose industrial output is expanding fast.

The Soviet wage-cost index is significantly below any of the others. However, the table should not be taken as an indication of the relative gains in standards of living in the various countries: while there were varying degrees of inflation in the non-Communist countries, retail prices actually fell significantly during the period in the USSR which added to the value of nominal wages.

The article quoted in *The Economist* is concerned with the rapid growth of the Japanese economy and of its competitive power in recent years. It points out that this is largely due to the more rapid growth of productivity than wages in Japan, and emphasises that this margin has enabled Japanese companies to attain an unusually high rate of capital accumulation. An important key to this is that, over the whole range of industry, trade unions are mostly weak and are often organized on a company basis rather than by industry or by craft. Thus, in certain important respects, conditions in the Japanese economy are strikingly similar to those in the Soviet economy and to what they were in the earlier days of the industrial era in most western economies such as Britain and the USA, when employers were not seriously confronted by organized labour.

Leaving aside the repulsiveness of a totalitarian economic system, what are its material disadvantages?

The basic defect of Soviet planning is that economic decisions are really political decisions. Development has been dogmatically determined and economic rationality subordinated to political expediency. Consumer sovereignty and the free play of supply and demand would limit the area of politico-economic decision making, so these normal guides to optimizing production have been discarded. This has led to a special kind of economic anarchy, and a frightening waste of resources. In other words, with prices arbitrarily fixed, widespread use of subsidies, and criticism either stifled or confined to officially approved subjects, there are not the same built-in disciplines as in a free economy. The relentless pursuit of political objectives combined with the lack of rational economic criteria has led to some particularly bad mistakes in investment.

Heavy industry is seen as an end in itself. In so far as it is essential to defence, and a country wishes to control its own supplies, nobody would quarrel with a decision to give it some measure of favoured treatment. However, the ideas of autarky and of metallurgy for its own sake have been taken to extremes throughout the Communist world. Every year, hundreds of millions of tons of coal and ore are being hauled by rail for journeys of several hundred miles to feed huge enterprises which, in a free economy, would go bankrupt. Rather than purchase the bulk of certain metals outside the bloc or so as to force the development of industries favoured by the planners, investments are undertaken to exploit the most unsuitable and intractable of raw materials. Examples of this are the unsuccessful and costly attempts in East Germany and Hungary to produce metallurgical coke from brown coal and, in the former, pig iron from ore of a grade so low that its exploitation was never undertaken by the Nazi regime even in its most autarkic frame of mind. And in China, during the 'Great Leap Forward', there was the ill-fated attempt to create millions of tons of additional iron and steel making capacity in the form of 'backyard' plants. This was a particularly serious failure which contributed heavily to China's present economic predicament.

In the USSR itself, probably the worst but no means the only instance of a heavy investment in the iron and steel industry which could not have been undertaken by private enterprise, or even by a democratic Government answerable to parliament, is that of the Cherepovets iron and steel works. Erection began shortly after the Second World War at a location over 300 miles east of Leningrad to meet the needs of the big engineering industry in and around the city. The necessary iron ore comes from the Kandalaksha region, nearly 900 miles away inside the Arctic circle. It was hoped that much of this would come by water, but the capacity of this route is limited and there is the problem of freezing during the winters. The coking coal comes entirely by rail from Vorkuta, also within the Arctic circle, but in a different direction, involving a haul of nearly 1,200 miles. Normally, undertakings such as this would be located on the coal and the ore fields so as to reduce transport costs by using loaded vehicles in each direction, but this is denied to Cherepovets; in addition, it is not particularly close to its main customers. In an ideal world, Leningrad would probably have got its iron and steel cheapest of all by importing most of it by sea from Belgium or Germany. A more economic alternative to Cherepovets would have been to restrict the growth of the engineering industry in Leningrad and to develop it in regions where iron and steel could be obtained much less expensively. As it is, the works is a cause of great concern to the authorities, and it looks as if the investment in the Kandalaksha ore mines and treatment plant may have to be abandoned in favour of deposits several hundreds of miles to the south of Cherepovets. If this happens, production costs will continue to be extremely high not only by Western European but by Soviet standards because of the excessively long rail hauls still involved and the continued lack of return loads.[1]

Just as striking as the case of Cherepovets are some of the USSR's experiences with the aluminium industry. There are big deposits of the main raw material—bauxite—within the Soviet borders, but they are widely dispersed and by far the greater part have a low aluminium and high silica content, making them costly to exploit. There is good quality bauxite in Hungary and since 1945, the USSR has obtained large amounts from this source, though long rail hauls are involved. Before the introduction of the new rouble, the official price within the Soviet economy of 4,400 roubles a ton was, at the official rate of exchange, more than double the western market price.[2] The USSR has also begun to produce aluminium from nepheline, which has a much lower aluminium oxide and higher silica content than bauxite and necessitates the handling of a bigger volume of ore and the use of more complex equipment, all of which mean greater costs unless, as claimed, it affords valuable by-products. Private enterprise could not have contemplated large-scale production of aluminium under Soviet conditions, yet in 1960 the Soviet Union produced over 700,000 tons, which made it the world's second producer. It intends to produce more than double this amount in 1965.

Not the least interesting feature of the Soviet aluminium story is that the forcing of output is due partly to the official decision to encourage its use as a substitute for copper, a branch of Soviet metallurgy which has caused considerable disappointment for many years. Yet, according to Kowalewski, when the Soviet aluminium price was over double the western price, that of copper was only 1.7 times, which would seem to indicate that copper might have been the better candidate for the more rapid development. The same authority cites even more striking instances of the disparity between

[1] Fairly recent figures show that treated ore cost 102 old roubles a ton in Cherepovets compared with 20 roubles in Magnitogorsk and 28 in Kuznetsk. Coke cost 202 old roubles a ton in Cherepovets against 160 in Magnitogorsk and 106 in Kuznetsk. Like Cherepovets, Magnitogorsk has to obtain coking coal by a long rail haul (1,125 miles from Kuznetsk). Costs in Ukraine are not available. As a whole they should be much lower than in Magnitogorsk because Krivoy Rog ore and Donetz coal are only about 300 miles apart.

[2] The Soviet price is quoted from Jan Kowalewski in the issue of *Optima* for December 1959. It is equivalent to £393 a ton at the official exchange rate then in force and compares with £180 a ton in the West (Metal Bulletin, October 16, 1959). This is not an exaggeration. According to the official Soviet Handbook of Prices for Construction Materials and Equipment for 1955, primary aluminium was priced at 4,700 to 6,000 old roubles a ton free on rail at producing works. There is no mention of aluminium in the revised list of metal prices issued in 1958.

Soviet and world prices for various other metals, with Soviet zinc, nickel, lead, tin and cobalt prices 4, 3.1, 7.6, 9.7 and 10.3 times the respective world prices.

These examples give some idea of the price of Soviet industrial progress, but it is not the end. The Communist system of emphasizing increased production rather than the earning of profits leads to two further drawbacks, both associated with the practice of awarding bonuses to workers and managers for the overfulfilment of production plans. First, a premium is automatically placed on poor quality, and secondly, it encourages widespread fraud, notably in the rendering of production returns. However, where it is essential, as with modern weapons and space vehicles, high quality production can be achieved. But it is long before production reaches the stage of consumer goods that quality becomes a consideration secondary to earning the bonus. Goods which in a non-Communist economy would be unsaleable because of their cost, poor quality or unsuitability, can be foisted on the customer because there is no alternative.

Visitors to the USSR are surprised by the shabby appearance both of the people and of the new blocks of flats. It is arguable that this poor quality is a normal feature of newly developing countries but, in comparison with Africa or Asia, the USSR was already appreciably developed before the first World War. Moreover, as Naum Jasny points out, in consumer goods and housing 'there has been deterioration, in many cases serious deterioration, compared with those products before the start of the Great Industrialization Drive.[1] Even so, many of them were at that time inferior in quality to those before the Revolution. The quality of many goods produced is thus greatly below that of fifty or sixty years ago.' He places only part of the blame for this on the direct producers, who are, in any case, prevented from producing high quality because of the poor raw materials and machinery at their disposal.[2]

The practice of rendering fraudulent production returns is encountered throughout the Communist world. It poses a particularly serious problem in the USSR where, in 1961, it became punishable by prison sentences of up to three years.[3] It involves not only direct falsification, but a great variety of ruses varying with the nature of the work. It is doubtful whether the 1961 legislation will succeed in more than scratching at the surface of the problem, because so many

---

[1] The Great Industrial Drive began in 1928.
[2] The Price of Soviet Industrialization, *Current History*, November 1961.
[3] *Pravda*, May 25, 1961.

people—workers, managers, inspectors, party—and other officials are involved. Indeed, it is probably true that without a certain measure of corruption the cumbersome bureaucratic system could never work and that fraud for some people is a matter of sheer survival. Allied to this is the other widespread practice in publicly-owned enterprises of concentrating on the overfulfilment of production plans for easily produced items to the detriment of those for the more difficult products. This may yield easy bonuses, but it causes great difficulties in other concerns both in industry and in agriculture, creating surpluses of certain items and a scarcity of others. The provision and installation of new equipment can be held up for several years because of the lack of essential components. Similarly, makers of machinery and equipment tend to be more interested in producing record numbers of their main products than in providing the spares needed to keep their previous years' deliveries in operation. The result is that the customer, whether a farm or works, has to choose between leaving machinery to rust, making the components itself inadequately and at high cost or obtaining them on the black market at inflated prices.

A further hazard is that the size and complexity of the economy complicates the distribution of finished products: the problem of maintaining the flow of industrial supplies is one of the most intractable in the Soviet Union. Rigid centralization is also partly to blame —no inducement is given to enterprise managers to adjust their output to customers' demands. This, too, becomes wasteful and situations constantly occur in which, for example, millions of yards of cloth are produced which are never sold simply because nobody wants what the planners think they want.

Agriculture has problems of its own. In contrast to the small farms which they mostly superseded, not only in the USSR but in Eastern Europe, the collective and State farms were expected to enjoy the advantages of large-scale operations. When the units are large, it is possible to invest in machinery and equipment which small peasant proprietors cannot afford; there are also important economies from the division of labour. Despite the advantages, many of them clearly indicated by the great and extensive private farms of North America, Communist agriculture has failed. It would appear that the key to success lies in private ownership. Whereas most people work relatively well in industry without owning the undertaking in which they are employed, an agriculture in which nobody owns anything apart from his small private plot cannot be satisfactorily operated. This can be illustrated by two examples from Eastern Europe. In Poland, since 1956, the authorities have been compelled to allow most collectives to revert to private owner-ship, and the food situation has substantially improved despite the conservative methods of the small farmers. In East Germany there has been an almost catastrophic worsening of the agricultural situation since collectivization was pushed to the limit in the early months of 1960, which is reflected in serious food shortages which had to be relieved by increased imports.

It has long been clear that farming lends itself far less readily to central planning than does industry, with the possible exception of the industrial branches such as sugar beet and raw cotton production. Moreover, owing to the vast acreages, it is impossible to secure anything like the same supervision of workers as is possible even in the largest industrial establishment. So, as far as food and fodder crops and livestock produce are concerned, the tale is one of pro-longed disappointments only occasionally relieved by a bumper year, when nature raises official hopes only to dash them again later.

The problems of Communism's agriculture are thus seen to be much greater than those of its industry. Whereas industry under Communism can justifiably claim to be expanding more quickly than that of some of the more advanced north Atlantic countries, no such claim can be made by its agriculture. It follows that as long as millions of people in Communist countries remain on the land with little to show for their being there, industrial output will also be lower than it need be. The full employment about which so much is made in the USSR is nothing more nor less than a mark of inefficiency. Until the problem of the low productivity per agricultural worker in the Communist world is solved, so that the greater part of the agri-cultural labour force can, as in the USA, migrate to industry, it is optimistic to talk of overtaking the industrial output per head of population of the leading democratic economies. However, just because there is a tremendous potential reserve of labour for industry in the Communist countryside, it is always possible that some day it may be drawn upon to the full.

If the supply of fertilizers, insecticides, machinery, equipment and buildings available to Communist agriculture could be increased to levels comparable with North America and Western Europe and, very important, if the provision of spare parts were adequate, there would be quite a different story, even under the system of collective and State farms. However, the Communist authorities are so dazzled by the prospects of heavy industrial development that they seem unable to bring themselves to spare adequate investment funds for agriculture and the supporting industries. This reluctance is probably due, in no small degree, to the preference of the Communist politician for industry and his antipathy to the individualism of the peasant. The preference for industry is to be found throughout the bloc, and the mutual distrust between the farming population and the government is most marked in the USSR and Eastern Europe.

Whether all the faults of the Communist form of economy are balanced by its virtues depends on the objective. If the standard set is that of being able to increase gross industrial output as fast as possible the advantages of the centrally-planned Communist economy are great. The chief are the ability to raise a very high proportion of the national product as savings without having to attract the private investor or to consider the taxpayer; the ability to direct these investments into the growth sectors without having to answer too many awkward questions from an electorate more interested in present amenities than in impressive production statistics; and the ability once enjoyed by the employer of Dickensian days of being able largely to ignore the desire of the worker for a bigger share in the proceeds of his labour. Against these advantages must be set the disadvantages of colossal muddle and waste; the high cost, low quality characteristic of much of the output and the failure to do more with agriculture than to exploit it as an ailing milch cow permanently hovering on the verge of death and requiring a disproportionate share of the labour supply to keep it functioning.

The disadvantages seem a heavy price to pay for the advantages. Growth may have been rapid in some sectors, but the sheer irrationality and inefficiency of much of this development hardly fits the Soviet Union, or most other Communist countries, for a competitive role in the world economy.

CHAPTER VI

Some Aspects of Growth in the Soviet Economy

The main standard set by Communist governments in judging the state of health of their economies is the speed at which output is growing. In the older industrial countries, before anybody thought the criterion of national economic achievement was to increase production faster than rivals, people were more inclined to think in terms of general prosperity, such as rising profits and real wages, or full employment. These benefits were the result of good business and usually meant that production would be growing fast; but it was not a case of output for output's sake. What mattered was that production should be matched by effective demand. In a western economy, the aim is a balanced development rather than a headlong rush; this is partly built into the system, and partly a matter of historical circumstance. In a country like the Soviet Union there are still large areas of unsatisfied demand which need to, and can, absorb quickly a rapidly increasing output. Some western observers, however, alarmed by the apparent speed of economic growth in Communist countries, tend to apply the same criterion to criticise the comparative stagnation of their own countries. Enough has been seen by now to indicate the weakness of such comparisons. We shall now look in more detail at the current performance of the Soviet economy.

The USSR is now engaged in completing the Seven Year Plan which began in 1959. It was claimed that this plan would lead to such an increase in the industrial output per head of population that, by 1965, it would exceed that of Britain and West Germany, while under the Twenty Year Programme (1960–1980) it would exceed that of the USA by 1970. Not surprisingly, the Twenty Year Programme figures have yet to be given in anything but the broadest outline. The main lines of development mapped out by these plans are summarized in the table overleaf.

The picture so far is of impressive industrial growth contrasting

D

SOVIET ECONOMIC DEVELOPMENT UNDER THE SEVEN-YEAR AND TWENTY-YEAR 'PLANS'

	Units	Claimed Development						Planned Development		
		1958	1959	1960	1961	1962	1963	1965	1970	1980
Industry										
Total Gross Output	Thousand million roubles	127	141	155	169	185	201	229	408	970–1,000
Producer Goods	„	85	95	105	116	128	141	160	287	720– 740
Consumer Goods	„	42	46	50	53	57	60	69	121	250– 260
Employment	Million persons	19.7	20.2	22.3	23.5	24.3	25.2	23.6	29.4	34.7
Labour Productivity	Index	100	107	113	118	125	131	145–150	226	463
Agriculture										
Total Gross Output	Thousand million roubles	48.5	48.7	49.8	51.3	51.9	47.5	80	124	174
Employment†	Million persons	34.1	33.3	32.3	31.4	31.0	30.5*	...	30.0	20.5
Labour Productivity	Index	100	103	108	115	118	109	190‡	290	600

* Estimated.
† Annual average, including workers on private plots.
‡ On collective farms to increase by 100 per cent and on state farms by 60 to 65 per cent.

sharply with almost total failure in agriculture. Industrial output is claimed to have risen by 58 per cent by the end of 1963 compared with 51 per cent planned, and by the end of 1965 the full 80 per cent seems likely to be achieved. In agriculture, however, results are discouraging: in the first four years of the plan there was a marginal rise in output amounting to less than the population increase, while in 1963, as a result of the grain harvest failure and the consequent slaughter of livestock, production plunged to a level below that of 1958.

An interesting feature of the industrial success is that it is chiefly the result of the appearance of unexpectedly large labour supplies rather than any spectacular gains in worker productivity. And the overall success masks failures in individual sectors: while the output of crude steel and oil is well ahead of plan, building materials and chemicals are lagging badly. Such over- and under-fulfilments are not new phenomena. Every post-war plan in the USSR has been characterised by conspicuous failure to achieve the intended increase in agricultural output, growth of industrial employment well in excess of plan, and a rapid but uneven expansion of industry.

It is useful to view the progress claimed so far under the Seven-Year Plan in the light of what is to be expected during the first decade of the Twenty-Year Programme. In the case of gross industrial output, what is apparently being demanded is that it should rise by nearly 48 per cent between 1960 and 1965 and by over 78 per cent between 1965 and 1970. The indications are that the former of these two aims may be achieved, but the pace proposed for the remaining five years is so much faster as to throw considerable doubt on its feasibility. As in many other industrial countries, rates of growth have declined. In recent five-year periods, the growth officially claimed is shown in the table overleaf.

The big increase claimed for 1945–50 (Fourth Five-Year Plan) and for 1950–55 (Fifth Five-Year Plan), of 88 and 85 per cent, respectively were somewhat above original expectations, Nevertheless, the planning authorities, quite realistically, did not aim at more than a 65 per cent increase between 1955 and 1960 and subsequently scrapped the plan in favour of the Seven-Year Plan with its much less ambitious objectives for almost every branch of the economy. In the event, the level of gross industrial output claimed for 1960 was only slightly below what had been originally planned, while, as already shown, the 48 per cent increase aimed at between 1960 and 1965 does not seem likely to differ much from what will eventually be claimed. Why, in the face of all this, should it be thought that Soviet industry

can hope to secure an increase of as much as 78 per cent in its gross
output between 1965 and 1970?

For the quinquennial or yearly percentage rates of industrial
growth to diminish as markedly as they have done in the USSR during
the last dozen years is not a sign of failure. For one thing, planners
have concentrated in the past on exploiting, often wastefully, the
most accessible natural resources, and now that many of these are
approaching depletion, the economy is affected by the law of
diminishing returns. A sounder means of assessing the growth of

OFFICIALLY CLAIMED GROWTH OF SOVIET GROSS INDUSTRIAL OUTPUT

	Yearly Percentages	*Quinquennial Percentages*
1945–50		88
1951	16	
1952	12	
1953	12	
1954	13	
1955	12	
1950–55		85
1956	11	
1957	10	
1958	10	
1959	11	
1960	10	
1955–60		64
1961	9	
1962	9.5	
1963	8.5	
1960–65 Plan		48
1965–70 Plan	12.2	78

output is to use a normal index number spanning far longer than five
years. The post-war percentages claimed by the USSR have been con-
verted into such an index, with 1945 as the base year. The results are
shown in facing table.

While the quinquennial percentages were quickly falling, the
absolute increase in production implicit in these percentages was
steadily becoming greater. Thus, if the 1965 Plan were fulfilled,

although only 48 per cent would have been added to production since 1960 against 88 per cent between 1945 and 1950, the absolute increase would be over three times as great as during the earlier period. This is impressive progress, but the table also shows how huge is the demand of the Twenty-Year Programme for gross industrial output to increase by 78 per cent between 1965 and 1970, since it would require a further growth of the index by 674 points, compared with one of only 294 points from 1960 to 1965. The previous Soviet trend suggests, indeed, that the growth likely to be achieved between 1965 and 1970 may not be more than another 320 points, giving a quinquennial increase of 38 per cent rather than the 78 per cent demanded by Khrushchev.

Two factors which affect the rate of economic growth are changes in labour supply and changes in labour productivity. Can anything be said about these that could lead us to believe that a tremendous acceleration of Soviet economic expansion will, in fact, take place? The sixfold increase in industrial, and the three and a half fold increase in agricultural production forecast for 1961–80 is to accrue mainly from a very rapid rise in productivity: about 8 per cent a year

CLAIMED AND PLANNED INCREASES IN GROSS
INDUSTRIAL OUTPUT OF THE USSR

			Quinquennial Increase Per Cent	*1945=100*	*Index Number Quinquennial Increases of Index*
1950 Claim	..	..	88	188	88
1955 Claim	..	..	84	348	160
1960 Claim	..	..	64	570	222
1965 Plan ..	..	..	48	864	294
1970 Plan ..	..	..	78	1,538	674

in industry and 9 per cent in agriculture. The industrial labour force is expected to grow at only 2 per cent a year, and in agriculture the whole of the extra output is to be achieved by gains in productivity. These figures appear excessively optimistic, especially those for agriculture, where the past lack of investment, institutional structure and general apathy of the peasants hinder large increases in output per worker. In the decade 1950–60, agricultural productivity rose by only half the rate anticipated for the next twenty years. As far as industry is concerned, the annual increment in output per worker has shrunk considerably within the last dozen years.[1]

Awareness of these trends must be a considerable factor in the official Soviet policy of relentlessly piling on the pressure for more and more investment, for it is largely by investment in mechanization and automation that labour productivity rates can be raised. Here, too, the planners face problems. A characteristic of investment in the past has been a high re-productivity: priority was given to steel mills which produced steel for more steel mills and so on. This was implemented at the expense of improving life for the consumer which would have meant diverting funds to such investments as textile mills or housing. If the authorities are at all concerned to fulfil their promise of giving the Soviet Union the highest standard of living in the world, then an increasingly large share of investment must go on items that do not reproduce themselves. Another factor is that as the economy matures, the replacement needs in the composition of investment increase; this naturally diminishes the ratio of output to investment.

Total investment in the economy is slightly ahead of the Seven-Year Plan. But more important than the fulfilment of monetary plans is the failure to secure the timely completion of the physical installations required. The information published suggests that the planners are constantly discovering that their investments cost considerably more and take much longer to complete than allowed for. In 1961, the shortages of machinery, equipment, and building materials were serious enough, and the accumulated total of incomplete projects was so great that Khrushchev suggested that there should be a year's moratorium on the starting of new schemes. Many of the delays are to be measured in years rather than months. They are part of the costly muddle inherent in a system seeking to control every conceivable branch of the economy from the centre instead of allowing individual undertakings to be responsible for their own fate.

It is sometimes suggested that the Soviet Union will overcome its problems by the widespread use of automation, but there are also doubts here. Automation is simply defined as the use of machines to control other machines, but Soviet usage gives the term the widest

[1] The percentage increases (over the previous year) claimed for output per industrial worker have been as below:

1950	..	13	1954	..	8	1958	..	6	1962	..	6
1951	..	10	1955	..	9	1959	..	7	1963	..	5
1952	..	7	1956	..	7	1960	..	5			
1953	..	7	1957	..	7	1961	..	4			

possible connotation. It ranges from the introduction of separate automatic machines and simple remote control systems to the more typical western automation systems using electronic and computer control of production processes. Soviet official interest began to be revealed prominently in propaganda by the middle 1950s. At its outset, this propaganda was probably intended less to impress foreign countries than to stimulate interest within the Soviet Union itself in a development whose successful promotion the authorities rightly saw could provide a powerful stimulus to productivity. A Ministry was created early in 1956 to deal with it and with the development of instruments, computers and other equipment required for automation. Official hopes were high that it would develop so far during the Sixth Five-Year Plan that it would be possible to secure an average increase of 50 per cent in productivity per production worker in industry by 1960. So great was the external impact of this propaganda that some western observers got the impression that the USSR was moving well ahead of the USA and Western Europe in automation. Thanks to the wealth of technical and industrial publications from the USSR which have become readily available to other countries since the death of Stalin and to the exchange of visits with specialists of many kinds from all over the world, much more is known about Soviet automation than would have been deemed possible only a few years ago. What emerges is that the official hopes for the latter half of the 1950s were largely disappointed. The claimed increase in labour productivity of 35 per cent between 1955 and 1960, disappointing to the Soviet authorities but impressive to the westerner, was achieved by virtually the same means as the 44 per cent increase claimed between 1950 and 1955. By and large, the major western industrial countries continue to be well ahead of the USSR in the introduction of automation—and most of them are gaining ground. This is partly because the USSR is still so far behind in mechanization, which is an essential preliminary to automation, that it cannot yet introduce automation in many of her industries. Moreover, since automation is so costly and, compared with such a country as the USA, the USSR is short of the necessary capital for the investments involved, it cannot be expected to make the same progress. This shortage of capital is greatly aggravated both by the physical difficulties of the USSR due to geography, geology and climate and to the very nature of her economy. The former impose the need for big investment outlays, while the Soviet system, with its confusion and waste, deprives the economy of resources which could have swelled the effective investment programme. In addition, managements are loth to forfeit overfulfilment bonuses for more distant gains which can only be secured by temporarily suspending production while new equipment is installed. This is a chronic Soviet difficulty. While it may not have had serious direct effects on automation it is a big delaying factor in the preceding mechanization. Finally, the Soviet defence programme takes a huge slice out of the resources which could be devoted to investment. This can be seen not only in financial terms but in the shortages of instruments and electronic apparatus for other than defence and space programme work.

Only in engineering has Soviet automation had any real effect on labour productivity. Even here, the USSR does not claim an average output per worker of more than 70 per cent of that of the engineering worker in the USA. Nevertheless, the Soviet engineering industry has long enjoyed priority and the advantages of really large-scale and expanding demand essential to mass-production methods. In common with other countries, the automatic production line has proved especially suitable in the manufacture of motor vehicle engines and components and tractors and agricultural machinery, and by 1955 the USSR had over 200 lines. Special attention has been given by her designers to their use in the production of ball-bearings, pistons and gear wheels, the technique having been carried further than had been usual in the West. By the end of 1963 Soviet industry may have had over 1,200 automatic lines, but there is no reason to believe that they are more efficient than their western counterparts; in fact there is a good deal of evidence to the contrary. So much attention appears to have been devoted to production lines that subsidiary means of raising productivity have been neglected. While advocating more and more automatic lines as the main means of raising productivity, Soviet planners admit they have a need for other improvements, for increased numbers of automatic machines, and for machinery with programme and electronic controls. An important part of the plan for 1965 provides for several of the leading Soviet engineering plants—mainly motor vehicle engine, tractor and agricultural machinery producers—to be similarly equipped to their American and Western European counterparts. This will require many more automatic transfer lines and automatic machine tools than are at present in use. Considerable progress can be expected, but the evidence suggests that none of the works concerned will have reached anything like this standard of automation by the time specified.

In most other industries, the development and application of automation to process control is confined to two or three plants, and few, if any, of the schemes have progressed beyond the trial and prototype stage. The main exceptions are in the electricity generating industry and at oil wells, where remote control systems are in fairly wide use. In the case of power stations, some form of automatic control began before the Second World War both in the USSR and in the West. Oil-well control—a post-war development—is more extensively applied in the USA than it is in the USSR. Oil refinery control, which came later than that of the wells, is more advanced in the West than in the USSR where deficiencies in instruments have seriously hindered plans for an automatic refinery.

In the iron and steel industry, pre-treatment of ores, high top pressures to blast furnaces and big furnaces generally have been the main reasons for high productivity in smelting and steel-making. Automated control of some of these processes and of rolling mill operation are being tried, but the progress made so far has been less than in the USA and Western Europe. The Soviet authorities themselves do not claim labour productivity in this industry of as much as 60 per cent of that of the USA.

It is claimed that in the Soviet chemical industry, automation systems have been installed at ammonia, nitric acid and ammonium nitrate plants but, at the end of 1962, not all were in operation and none was in advance of those installed in the West during the past three years. The chemical industry in particular is one of those in which automation is being attempted when the general level of ordinary mechanization and instrumentation is limited and poor, thus depriving it of the conditions in which automation can be satisfactorily applied. The Soviet authorities themselves admit the industry has a labour productivity of only 40 per cent of that of the USA, while in synthetic rubber production Soviet labour productivity in 1956 was admitted to be as low as 17 per cent of the USA.

It would seem that the more rapid percentage growth of Soviet industrial labour productivity over that in Britain and the USA derives more from the backwardness of the former, which provides much leeway to be made good, than it does from the vaunted superiority of the Soviet system. A good deal of what is happening in Soviet industry today is still very much a matter of what happened in Britain and the USA before the First World War.

CHAPTER VII

Soviet Industry

Soviet industrial growth has so far been discussed in general terms, involving measurements both of total output and of productivity. In considering the growth of the individual industries which contribute to the general total, it is possible in most cases to use physical measurements. Taken together, these sometimes give a rather different impression of the official success story from that of the gross output index. Nevertheless, the USSR's industrial strength and her capacity to maintain a rapid rate of industrial growth are demonstrated by such sectors as energy production, iron and steel, and engineering—those industries, in fact, on which the authorities have lavished so much of their attention. These and other branches will be examined to give a more comprehensive picture of Soviet capabilities and prospects.

FUEL AND POWER INDUSTRIES

When the Sixth Five-Year Plan was scrapped as misconceived, it was recognized that one of the biggest errors of the Stalin era, still being made in the middle 1950s, was the excessive emphasis on coal, the relative neglect of oil and the great neglect indeed of natural gas. The substitution of the latter two for coal would afford big economies in labour and transport and greatly reduce consumption losses. Much of the current plan is therefore concerned with a thorough-going change of emphasis of the energy supply. The table which follows shows the change in emphasis intended and progress made so far.

For primary energy as a whole, the original plan set out to increase the output from 622 million tons of standard fuel in 1958 to just over 1,000 million tons in 1965, or by 63 per cent. Out of these

SOVIET ENERGY OUTPUT

	Unit	1953	1958	1959	1960	1961	1962	1963	1965 New Plan	1965 Old Plan
Hard Coal	Million metric tons	224.3	353.0	365.4	374.9	377.0	386.4	400*	420*	438*
Brown Coal	,,	96.1	143.1	141.4	138.3	133.5	131.0	132*	133*	168*
Crude Oil	,,	52.8	113.2	129.6	147.9	166.1	186.2	205.5	240	230–240
Natural Gas	Thousand million cu. m.	6.9	28.1	35.4	45.3	59.0	73.5	89.5	125.5	148
Peat	Million metric tons	38.6	53.3	60.5	53.6	51.6	34.7	30*	20*	20*
Shale	,,	6.1	13.2	13.7	14.1	15.2	16.4	18*	20*	20*
Firewood	Million cu. m.	112.2	124.1	127.7	108.0	97.7	97.0	95*	90*	90*
Hydro-electricity	Thousand million kWh	19.2	46.5	47.6	58.0	59.0	66.8	75*	100*	100*
Total Primary Energy	Million metric tons standard fuel†	386.6	622.1	665.3	699.9	740.1	787.9	849.0*	957*	1,001–1,015*
Coke	Million tons	36.9	50.9	53.4	56.2	58.6	60.9	67.0	76–80*	76–80*
Total electricity	Thousand million kWh	134.3	235.4	265.1	292	327	369	412	508	520

* Estimated.

† Standard fuel is used to express in uniform terms the varying energy content of different fuels and contains 7,000 kilocalories per kilogramme. Soviet statistics indicate use of the following equivalents for the energy sources listed above, though the rates may vary slightly from year to year:

hard coal (per ton)	0.83 tons of standard fuel	peat (per ton)		0.38 tons of standard fuel
brown coal (per ton)	0.46 ,, ,, ,, ,,	shale (per ton)		0.34 ,, ,, ,, ,,
crude oil (per ton)	1.43 ,, ,, ,, ,,	firewood (cu. m.)		0.32 ,, ,, ,, ,,
natural gas (per 1,000 cu. m.)	1.20 ,, ,, ,, ,,	hydro-electricity (per kWh)		0.12 ,, ,, ,, ,,

totals the amount consumed by industry was to rise from 277 million tons to 485 million or by 75 per cent. This was one of the bases for the planned increase of 80 per cent in gross industrial production. It is roughly consistent with recent Soviet experience. Thus, in 1960, when gross industrial output was claimed as 64 per cent above that of 1955, primary energy output had risen by only 45 per cent. The increase in industrial consumption of energy during these years is not precisely known, but it was certainly less than the former figure though clearly more than the latter. Since gross industrial output is planned to grow faster than primary energy output, of which, moreover, a small but increasing proportion is exported, it would appear that some allowance for the substitution of the more efficient oil and gas for the more wasteful solid fuels has been made in the Seven-Year Plan.

However, to secure the intended supply of primary energy is not proving easy. Whereas between 1953 and 1958 the average annual increase in the total output of primary energy was 47 million tons of standard fuel, an average of 55-60 million was at first demanded between 1958 and 1965. The figure achieved in the five years since 1958 was about 45 million which, under the original plan, would have involved a mean increase of some 80-85 million for 1964 and 1965. To double the previous average in the last two years of the plan may well have appeared unnecessary by the end of 1963, owing to the hope of reducing the waste of oil and gas. In any case it must also have appeared impossible. Accordingly, reduced plans for coal and gas were announced in the Plenum of December 1963, the effect of which was to lower the primary energy objective for 1965 by roughly 5 per cent, or some 50 million tons of standard fuel. The mean increase required in the next two years then fell from 80-85 million to the more realistic figure of about 54 million tons.

Coal

Under the original Seven-Year Plan hard and brown coal output was supposed to increase by an average of 15.7 million tons a year until 1965. Compared with yearly increases in the 1950s of between 20 and 30 million tons this is modest for the USSR, but the average since 1958 has been little over 7 million tons, with output actually falling in 1961. Three-quarters of the coal produced is hard coal, the rest being brown coal of little more than half the energy value. Output of both types rose fast from the war years until 1958, but whereas that of hard coal has since then made continuous though slower progress, that of brown coal has slightly fallen and seems unlikely to rise appreciably until after 1965. This is because the deliberate restriction or closure of the uneconomic brown coal mines in the Moscow region has outpaced the exploitation of the low-cost opencast deposits in Siberia. By 1961 it seemed clear that the Soviet coal industry was no longer seriously trying to reach its original 1965 objective of 600-612 million tons, but it was not until the Plenum of December 1963 that the new and sharply reduced plan of 553 million tons was announced. The respective shares of hard and brown coal in this total were not mentioned but more hard coal of the coking grades is urgently needed and the cuts seem to have fallen chiefly on brown coal.

The timing of this announcement seems to preclude the idea that the Soviet planners had suddenly switched over to oil and gas. The original plan prescribed ambitious objectives for both these fuels, but whereas that of oil still stands and may be reached with a little to spare, that of gas has been even more drastically cut than that of coal. The main reason for the reduction seems to be that demand for furnace as distinct from coking coal was over-estimated at the start of the plan and that even in 1959 huge stocks—mainly of power station grades and notably in the Donets basin—were already in hand and have taken years to run down. By 1963 the authorities must have decided that much of the extra coal for which they had planned would not justify the cost of extraction, if only because the new power stations and other plants destined to burn it would not be ready in time. In any event the coal industry, still ravaged by the predatory and inefficient exploitation of earlier years, could scarcely have made good the whole leeway in the last two years of the plan period.

Oil

The plan laid down that crude oil output should increase from 113 million tons in 1958 to 240 million[1] in 1965. Actual output, according to Khrushchev, exceeded the planned total by over 22 million tons in the first five years, and even the plan is well above domestic requirements. From the outset the planners seem to have aimed at large exports. These have risen fast since 1955 and in 1963 amounted to some 50 million tons (including those to other bloc countries), or nearly a quarter of the year's production. Until recently it seemed likely that crude output would pass the 1965 plan

[1] Originally assumed as 230–240 million, but the lower figure dropped out of use as output rose. Perhaps significantly, it has recently reappeared.

by many million tons and that there would be a rapid and continuous growth in the export surplus.

As explained in Chapter XI the foreign trade position now looks less favourable. The output of 240 million tons intended for 1965 will probably be achieved but will only be exceeded by little, if anything. Prospecting and other field work has often been slow and misdirected and new reserves, however large and confidently claimed, are not being proved at the required rate. New refineries take too long to design and assemble and the whole refining apparatus, although in scale adequate to present need, lags behind the West in technique. The oil charged to refineries is often of intractable quality, and the resulting yield of refined products is none too well suited either to home or to export requirements. Oil pipeline construction, yielding precedence to gas, is far behind schedule and the same may well apply to other transmission and handling facilities. Finally consumption, no doubt inflated by the loss and waste occasioned by these shortcomings, has risen unduly fast and has led to shortages of certain products, notably diesel fuel. To cure these ills the oil and gas industries have been allotted 50 per cent more investment for 1964 and 1965 than for the previous two years, but the benefits are unlikely to be fully realised until later, when commitments will have further increased.

Natural Gas
Although still far less important than coal or oil in the Soviet energy pattern, the output of natural gas, insignificant until the late 1950s, has since grown much faster than either of these fuels. It has, however, consistently fallen short of expectation. This led the authorities to manipulate annual objectives until they were low enough to be exceeded, as in the past two years, although this, in turn, was bound to compromise the achievement of the Seven-Year Plan. Eventually, in December 1963 they reduced the plan by some 23,000 million cu. m. or about 15 per cent.

These evasions and partial failures are partly due to the poor field work and partly to the nature of the gas, which needs a chain of special installations from well to consumer before it can be used. In terms of pipelines laid or approaching completion the gas industry has been well served at the expense of oil, but most of the other links in the chain are defective or incomplete. Field installations to prepare the gas for transmission and conserve valuable liquids otherwise wasted are often lacking, and there are many reports of gas lost, flared off or wasted. Turbo-compressors, on which depends the rate of gas delivery through the pipelines, are scarce and some trunk lines are working well below capacity. Bulk storage at the large centres has been slow to develop, though by 1965 it may perhaps suffice for the lower output now envisaged. Lastly, the lack of local distribution facilities and appliances for direct use has retarded gas consumption. All these factors have tended to curtail output in the field. Gas, like oil, has for some time enjoyed an investment level above the average for Soviet industry and it should now benefit from the 50 per cent rise which it will share with oil. Nevertheless, its contribution to the Soviet energy pattern is rather less than had been hoped and will remain so at least until the end of the present plan.

Electricity
The original 1965 plan for electricity generation was 500-520 thousand million kWh. From time to time higher maxima were predicted, and as late as September, 1963, the forecast was over 520 thousand million. Only at the Plenum of December, 1963, was the firm figure of 508 thousand million announced. How far this figure represents a renunciation of earlier hopes is not clear. To reach it, however, output must grow on average by 48 thousand million kWh a year. On the strength of the achievements of 1959 and 1960 this seems unlikely, but there were increments of 35, 42 and 43 thousand million, respectively, in 1961, 1962 and 1963. Further significant increases in the annual increment will be needed in the remaining years for the 1965 plan to be fulfilled. Generating capacity is tight, and much depends on the ability to secure large-scale production and installation of the new 200 mW generators. Up to about two years ago, the general average capacity of generators produced was under 100 mW. The larger generators are now being successfully produced and much larger ones still are in prospect, so it should not be impossible to fulfil the plan for electricity generation in 1965. Investments in the industry have long been at a high level. At 1,580 million roubles in 1961 they were little more than 20 per cent higher than in 1956, but more than double the British investment in gas, electricity and water undertakings combined.

Despite the enormous investments in energy, on a whole it appears that the Soviet authorities have reduced their original energy plan for 1965 by about 5 per cent to the equivalent of roughly 950 million tons of standard fuel. There is no obvious reason why this should not be achieved. With the electricity plan standing a good chance of completion and oil and gas economical to use, this marginal failure does not necessarily entail an underfulfilment of the plan for gross industrial production. It does, however, suggest that painful readjustments may be necessary; for example, the expanded plan for the gas-consuming petrochemical industry, taken in conjunction with the sharply reduced supply of natural gas, must mean a severe pinch for some other sector of the economy. It also underlines the doubts about the feasibility of Khrushchev's much more ambitious general industrial plan for 1970.

THE METALLURGICAL INDUSTRIES

The iron and steel industry has always held the imagination of the Communists. There is something of a mystical symbolism about the words, with their implication of military strength, and the effort put into promoting production is undertaken with almost the same enthusiasm as is devoted to armaments and the conquest of space. The Sixth Five-Year Plan (1956–60) envisaged increases in production and investment larger than those achieved in any of its predecessors, and it emphasised the expansion of iron and steel as the basis for industrial development generally in the regions beyond the Urals. One of the main reasons for its failure was the impossibility of carrying out the programme for the metallurgical industry, particularly in mining and beneficiation of iron ore.

The Seven-Year Plan, which succeeded it in 1959, although far from unambitious, benefited initially from the completion of capital construction projects begun some years before. It was also more realistic since, while paying lip-service to the long-term schemes for developing the eastern regions, it redirected effort to the older metallurgical centres of the Urals and the European part of the USSR, whose reserves of manpower, materials and technical skill promised quicker and cheaper returns. The change of emphasis was reflected in the pattern of investment. Although the planned amount for 1959–65 was 2.4 times as great as actual investment in the previous seven years, nearly two-thirds of it was to be devoted to the expansion and modernization of existing enterprises. Less than 25 per cent of the planned increases in production was to come from new plants.

There was a good start, and the annual plans for the first two years were comfortably exceeded, somewhat to the surprise, it would seem, of the planning authorities themselves. Although there was some slight underfulfilment in 1961, output of steel was still increasing at an average annual rate of 9 per cent, compared with approximately

7 per cent, as originally intended. Towards the end of that year Khrushchev announced revised objectives for 1965. Production of steel was to reach 95–97 million tons, instead of 86-91 million tons, implying an average annual increase of 8 per cent for the rest of the plan, a rate which seemed perfectly feasible in the light of progress so far. Khrushchev also announced goals for steel production in 1970 and 1980, of 145 million tons and 250 million tons, respectively.

In 1962, however, there were signs of a slowing-down, the annual plans both for pig iron and crude steel being significantly under-fulfilled. Late in the year, the 1965 objectives were again revised—downwards this time to about their original level. The goals for 1963 reflected these changes by calling for a substantially lower rate of increase—only 5 per cent in the case of steel—than in any previous year of the Seven-Year Plan.

It is a matter of conjecture whether this was merely a change of policy or a recognition of shortcomings within the industry itself. Soviet propaganda, with its suggestion that steel production was rising too fast and its emphasis on the competing claims of agriculture and the chemical industry, contrives to give the impression that the brake has been applied voluntarily; but there are grounds for believing that it would in any case have been applied automatically through continued delays in execution of production schedules. Warning symptoms had already appeared in the regular under-fulfilment of the annual investment plans. In the first two years of the Seven-Year Plan the deficiency averaged 7 per cent, and in 1961 and 1962, nearly 20 per cent. This somewhat resembles what took place in the mid-1950s. but whereas the most serious shortcomings then were in the iron ore industry and in iron-making capacity, the greatest threat to the maintenance of high output now lies in the failure to implement plans for the introduction of new steel-making capacity. For some time this failure was offset by improvements in technology and the increasing use of oxygen and natural gas. However, the introduction on a large scale of the Austrian oxygen converter or L.D. process, which is transforming the industry throughout the world and was progressively to replace the open-hearth furnace in the USSR, has not gone according to plan. By 1965, it was to yield about 20 million tons a year, but Soviet failure to master the process, means that it is unlikely to account for more than 5 million tons in that year. To make good the deficiency new open-hearth furnaces are being provided, although it had been announced that no more would be built after 1963.

In other branches of the industry, although much progress has

E

been made, many important projects remain well behind schedule. For example, in the rolling mill sector, there have been serious delays in the provision of modern equipment for the replacement of much obsolete capacity and the improvement in quality and range of rolled steel output. Production plans for finished steel as a whole are claimed to have been fulfilled, but the continued deficiences in certain types of product, especially cold-rolled sheets and strip, as well as a whole range of tubes needed for the oil, gas and chemical industries have embarrassed the rest of the economy.

The progress of non-ferrous metallurgy is difficult to assess, because of the persistent failure to publish absolute figures of production. Even percentage statements have been few and far between. Planned investment for the seven years is believed to have been slightly more than half the amount allocated to the iron and steel industry, 60 per cent of the total being devoted to the extension and reconstruction of existing enterprises. Although the annual investment plans for most of the metals have been underfulfilled, it has now been decided to make a supplementary grant of nearly 2,000 million roubles for the last two years of the plan.[1]

In the aluminium industry, expansion depends on a big building programme and new plants under construction in Siberia and Kazakhstan will provide a great proportion of the enlarged capacity required by 1965. Although an increase in production of 180-200 per cent is planned—the biggest for any non-ferrous metal—there seems to be little likelihood of this happening. The industry still depends partly on imported bauxite, mainly from Greece, but alternative, though costly, sources of aluminium within the Soviet Union should soon make imports of bauxite unnecessary.

Apart from its strategic importance and its versatility in civil use, one reason for the emphasis on aluminium is as a substitute for copper in the electrical industry. In spite of continued efforts to raise production to adequate levels, copper remains a deficiency metal. Long handicapped by obsolete equipment, it has been slow to develop an up-to-date technology. Recently, however, there has been evidence of increased facilities and improved techniques—especially in the mining and concentration of ores, which had previously lagged behind smelting and refining. The output of metal is believed to be proceeding now at a considerably higher rate than in the earlier years of the plan, as indeed it will need to do if the fairly ambitious goal for 1965 is to be attained.

In spite of having what are claimed to be the world's largest

[1] *Tsvetnye Metally*, No. 1, 1964.

reserves of lead and zinc, the Soviet Union occupies second place, at some distance behind the USA, as a producer of these metals. Although Soviet exports of both have figured recently in western markets, this may well be at some sacrifice of domestic needs. Nor does the unambitious nature of the current plans for expanding production afford grounds for believing that anything more than a finely-balanced self-sufficiency can be maintained in the foreseeable future.

Tin is the only major metal, apart from copper, of which the supply is certainly inadequate for domestic requirements. The size of Soviet reserves is not known, but most of the deposits lie in the remote and inhospitable regions of eastern Siberia, with possibly 25 per cent in the Yakutsk ASSR. The progress of tin mining in these regions has been very unsatisfactory, and recoveries of metal are notoriously low throughout the industry.

The following table gives statistics of metallurgical output, actual and planned. Those for the iron and steel industry are official Soviet figures; those for the non-ferrous metals are estimates.

SOVIET METALLURGICAL OUTPUT

	Unit	1958	1959	1960	1961	1962	1963	1965 Plan
Iron Ore	Million tons	88.8	94.4	107	118	128	137	
Pig Iron	,, ,,	39.6	43.0	46.8	50.9	55.5	58.7	65.7
Crude Steel	,, ,,	54.9	60.0	65.3	70.7	76.3	80.2	89.3
Finished Steel	,, ,,	43.1	47.0	50.9	55.2	59.2	62.4	69.0
Aluminium	Thousand tons	511.5	610	701.5	807	945	1105	1430–1530
Copper	,, ,,	429	450.5	490	529	571	639	815
Lead	,, ,,	250	265	280	297	315	334	370
Zinc	,, ,,	300	320	345	370	396	424	480
Tin	,, ,,	20	21	22	23	24	25.5	30

THE ENGINEERING INDUSTRIES

The engineering industries as a whole comprise the largest of all the USSR's industrial groupings and account for over 20 per cent of its industrial capital. They are closely related to armaments production, the practice being, in peace-time as well as in war, to devote many of the more important plants both to defence and to civil production. The official figures of gross industrial output and of engineering output, both of necessity calculated in roubles, are always understood to include armaments. The Seven-Year Plan is for engineering output to be double the 1958 amount by 1965, for which a yearly

increase averaging just over 10 per cent is implied. The annual
percentage increases claimed so far have been as follows:

1959—15; 1960—16; 1961—16; 1962—15; 1963—13.

All the above substantially exceed 10 per cent and would, in fact,
support a claim that output in 1963 was already at the level originally
planned for 1965. Moreover, State investments in the engineering
industry up to the end of 1961 reached a volume well above the
yearly average intended in the Seven-Year Plan. This was for 11,740
million roubles for the whole period, or an average of 1,677 million
a year. In 1961 alone an investment of 1,991 million was claimed,
although in 1962 and 1963 the growth of investments in the industries has been much more modest than in preceding years.

The figures published on individual branches indicate, as might
be expected, a rapid growth, but hardly a doubling of the output
between 1958 and 1963. While many products are claimed to have
had an output in 1963 at least double that of 1958, there are considerably more for which this claim has not been made. Moreover,
the overwhelming proportion of the latter appear unlikely to double
their output during the seven years. This is, of course, a rough and
ready assessment, for it was never intended to double the output of
each individual item. Nor is it possible to allow accurately for
individual values or weights. However, there are some important
and costly products whose output is well ahead of the general
schedule, notably transformers and generators, which are always
urgently needed, instruments, which are essential both to defence
and to automation, and chemical equipment. Since the Seven-Year
Plan was inaugurated more attention than ever has been focused on
increasing the production of chemical plant, but there are many
difficulties to overcome and the USSR has further stepped up the plan
for this branch of the industry besides trying to increase its foreign
purchases. Other important engineering items whose output is well
ahead of the general schedule are diesel locomotives and turbines.

The more slowly advancing products include such important items
as machine tools, forging and pressing tools, metallurgical equipment, rolling stock, motor vehicles, a great deal of agricultural
machinery, anti-friction bearings and petroleum equipment. In
several cases a drop in output is admitted and in others it can be
assumed. It would be wrong, however, to attribute the apparent
discrepancy between the individual production figures and the total
for the whole engineering industry to the rendering of fraudulent

output returns. This type of cheating is traditional and is unlikely to have increased significantly in five years. A more likely conclusion is that while Soviet engineering output is growing fast, its rapidly changing emphasis and the peculiarities of its artificial price structure are exaggerating its real rate of growth. It could also be that a faster growth in the output of armaments than was originally planned has been holding back the growth in a number of the civil departments of the industry.

An interesting aspect is the modest volume of Soviet compared with American and British output of motor vehicles and consumer goods, despite the huge size of the Soviet engineering industry and Khrushchev's repeated promises to improve consumer supplies.

OUTPUT IN 1962

Item	Unit	USSR	USA Output	Per Cent of USSR	UK Output	Per Cent of USSR
Cars	Thousands	166	6,900	4,160	1,250	750
Lorries and Buses	,,	412	1,240	300	425	103
Wireless Sets	,,	4,250	19,200	450	2,976	70
TV Sets	,,	2,170	6,500	300	1,463†	67
Refrigerators	,,	838	4,865*	580	720‡	86
Washing Machines	,,	1,800	6,485	360	1,102	61

* Including 1,090,000 'deep freezes'.
† In 1959 production was 2,863,000.
‡ Estimated on value basis.

The American motor vehicle industry completely dwarfs that of the USSR, particularly in the case of passenger cars, but even British car output was more than seven times the Soviet and, in 1962, British output of commercial vehicles exceeded that of the USSR, despite the greater Soviet emphasis on this branch. It will be pointed out that the USSR relies far more than do the USA and Britain on railways, to which the reply can be made that the latter regard this as a largely outmoded form of transport. Nor does it speak well of the Soviet road system.

In the case of domestic appliances, the much greater American and British emphasis is again striking. Although the population of the USA is only 86 per cent of that of the USSR and has long enjoyed widespread use of such things as wireless sets, refrigerators and washing machines, American output is 4.5, 5.8 and 3.6 times respectively that of the USSR. Comparison with Britain is also unfavourable.

Per head of population, the British output of wireless sets is 2.9 times that of the USSR, 2.8 times for television receivers, 3.6 times for refrigerators and 2.6 times for washing machines. The comparison does not end there. The quality of most of the Soviet consumer goods is so poor that they would be unsaleable on the American or British markets. Furthermore, the comparisons have been limited to the very items for which figures are available. Many other products are taken for granted in the average American or many a British household but are scarcely to be seen in Soviet homes. These include lawn mowers, electric food mixers, dishwashers, water softeners, waste disposers and mechanical toys of all kinds.

This Anglo-American, indeed, Western European, emphasis on consumer goods is the direct result of allowing private individuals to have as much say as they still do, even in the 1960s, in determining the pattern of industrial production. In an era when the standard is not present-day consumer satisfaction, but growth rates and the satisfaction of consumers yet unborn, to devote so much to the current production of consumer goods is sometimes regarded as a weakness. The small Soviet output of such items as household equipment is a reflection of the emphasis laid on 'producer goods' and armaments, and the whole policy of trying to outstrip the USA both in military strength and in industrial output per head of population within the present decade. If armaments production did not absorb so high a proportion of the engineering industry's best human and material capacity as it does, the prospect of overtaking the USA industrially would be greatly enhanced. Much greater, too, would be the Soviet potentiality in the production of capital equipment for African, Asian and Latin American countries.

THE CHEMICAL INDUSTRY

In spite of its importance in national defence, the Soviet chemical industry was so neglected up to 1958 as almost to be one of the Cinderellas of the economy. This is not to underestimate its size, particularly on the inorganic side, but it bore all the traces of a neglected industry—old-fashioned run-down plants, poor quality products and out-of-date techniques. The tremendous advances in the West since 1945 on the petrochemical side had almost passed the USSR by. In 1958 the picture changed dramatically. Khrushchev had promised substantial improvements in the supply of consumer goods and the standard of housing, and he realized that development of plastics and chemical fibres could have rapid effects. He was faced with tremendous problems of re-equipping and re-vitalizing a backward industry and his plans for 1965 were to prove quite unattainable. Nevertheless, the next five years saw a rapid rise in chemical investment and output, and a large-scale changeover to petroleum hydrocarbon feedstocks.

In retrospect, the Plenum on the chemical industry in May 1958 must be viewed as a turning point in Soviet industrial development. But Khrushchev over-extended himself, and the Achilles-heel, as usual, was agriculture. He was hoping to meet the increasing food demand by an expansionist policy in agriculture, at the same time gradually intensifying production by development of the mineral fertilizer and pesticide industries through his chemical programme. His luck held surprisingly well, but the situation was bound to come to a head as the initial fertility of the Virgin Lands became exhausted and climatic factors intervened.

The emphasis now being laid, belatedly but wisely, on the intensification of agriculture will slow down the chemical advance as a whole. At the Plenum in December 1963, Khrushchev's ambitious 1965 plans for plastics, fibres and tyres were scaled down, as was the whole chemical plan, so as to concentrate on fertilizers and pesticides. As far as 1970 is concerned, the plastics plan has been lowered—it was anyway very high—but Khrushchev is clearly hoping that his resources can cope with a still ambitious programme in such products as fibres, rubber and tyres, alongside the concentration on agricultural chemicals. The strain on the economy, particularly the engineering industries, will be immense, and even viewing the chemical industry in isolation, the available construction facilities are wholly inadequate for such a programme. Khrushchev might have another run of luck, but if there were to be a further failure of the harvest in, say, 1965 or 1966, some of the chemical plans for 1970 might have to be modified.

Sulphuric acid production is a good indicator of the size and growth of the traditional chemical industry. At 6.9 million tons in 1963, the USSR ranked second in the world, but its output was nevertheless only about a third that of the USA. It is probable that the 1965 Plan for sulphuric acid has been slightly reduced, but even if it were fulfilled, output would be rather less than two-thirds of America's present production. The available evidence suggests that the plan will not be fulfilled, although the rate of increase accelerated considerably in 1963. The industry is facing considerable technological changes which have not been proceeding very fast and much of the existing equipment is poor and frequently breaks down. About a third of the total production is absorbed by superphosphates, but this is far short of what is needed.

Agricultural chemicals are now enjoying high priority because of the recent decision to intensify agriculture. One of the most important aspects of the December 1963 Plenum was that Khrushchev appears to have turned away from a possible expansion of the agricultural area northwards in favour of meeting what has been Soviet agriculture's greatest need, a large-scale programme to restore and improve the fertility of the old lands. The consumption of mineral fertilizers per hectare of arable land in the USSR is extremely low in terms of nutrient value, 13.1 kgs. in 1962 compared with 40.3 kgs. in the USA and over 180 kgs. in Britain. The USSR hopes to raise her consumption to 29 kgs. in 1965 and about 70 kgs. by 1970, but is facing

SOVIET CHEMICAL AND RUBBER OUTPUT

	Unit	1953	1958	1962	1963	1965 Plan New	1965 Plan Old	1970 Plan
Sulphuric Acid	Thousand tons	2,919	4,803	6,132	6,887	...	11,288	...
Mineral Fertilizers	„ (bulk)	6,968	12,420	17,262	19,900	35,000	35,000	70–80,000
Mineral Fertilizers	„ (nutrient weight)	...	2,950	4,080	4,660	8,160	...	19,060
Plastics	„	...	260	475	589	950	1,700	3,500–4,000
Synthetic Rubber*	„	...	191	263	390	...	710	...
Motor Tyres	Million	8.1	14.4	20.8	22.6	26	29	44
Chemical Fibres	Thousand tons	62.3	166	277.3	308	444	666	1,350

* Estimates.

tremendous problems, not just in production but in achieving the correct and scientific application of fertilizers. In terms of nutrient weight, the production of the three main types is probably still no more than half that of the USA. The main advance since 1958 has been with nitrogenous fertilizers, but the quality of both superphosphate and potash is poor. Nevertheless, the investment now being channelled to this industry will bring substantial increases in capacity, production and quality over the next seven years, and output of mineral fertilizers as a whole in 1965 is unlikely to be less than 29–30 million tons, compared with the plan of 35 million tons. These huge quantities will create problems of their own, notably in transport, packaging and actual application by the conservative peasantry. Colossal waste is to be expected.

One of the most striking aspects of Soviet chemicals is the late development of the petrochemical industry. A principal feature of the Seven-Year Plan—and from a longer-term point of view probably the most important—is the changeover in raw material base, from traditional by-products of the coke and timber industries and agriculture to petroleum hydrocarbons. Thus industries associated with petrochemicals—plastics, synthetic rubber, synthetic fibres and synthetic alcohol—were allocated over half the investment planned for chemicals as a whole. It was hardly likely that the changeover would proceed smoothly in all cases. Petrochemical plants have been constructed before their supply of raw materials from oil refineries and natural gas processing stations was available. There was also the question of techniques. Many of the processing techniques used in petrochemicals in the West have been taken from modern oil refinery technology, a field where the USSR was notably backward. Extensive help from the West has been sought and is likely to continue, however, and has undoubtedly eased the difficulties. The changeover has been impressive in the nitrogen industry, for example, and is gaining momentum in plastics and synthetic fibres.

Output of plastics has been growing fast under Khrushchev's blessing, and again much plant has been bought from the West, but the emphasis on fertilizers may impede progress and both the 1965 and 1970 plans have been scaled down, though they were extremely ambitious. The structure of Soviet output will be different from that in the USA for some time, the older plastics being more dominant, and America will certainly not be overtaken by 1970. It remains difficult to say how much the private consumer will benefit from the development, for example, of a large-scale polyethylene (polythene) industry, as the potential demand of industry and agriculture is immense. This is not true of chemical fibres, which have certain industrial uses, as in tyres, but are clearly associated with Khrushchev's aim to improve the standard of living. Clothing in the main cities, at least, and for the higher income groups has already benefited.

The synthetic rubber industry is old-established. The USSR was producing artificial rubber long before the Germans and Americans became seriously interested, but despite this lead, the story is one of repeated failure to fulfil plans, difficulties in using the product, and heavy costs. Production is now running at above 400,000 tons a year —a long way from the USA's output of 1.6 million tons in 1962. The USSR is trying to telescope within seven years the changeover from a pre-1940 type rubber to that now commonly used in the West and, between 1963 and 1965, to move into the new stereo-rubbers. It is hardly surprising that difficulties have been encountered and the new rubbers are still not in large-scale production. Imports of natural rubber may decline somewhat, but it is hard to believe that they can fall much below 250,000 tons a year up to 1970.

Khrushchev has vastly increased the allocation of investments to the chemical industry but in no year since 1958 has it been fully absorbed. After a great spurt in 1959 and 1960, the tempo of investments quickened again in 1963, but the plans for the next two years are extremely ambitious. The relevant figures for the so-called centralized investment are as follows:

INVESTMENT IN CHEMICAL INDUSTRY
(million roubles)

Year	Planned	Actual Amount	Increase
1958	...	447	140*
1959	760*	698	251
1960	950*	915	217
1961	1,278	1,070	155
1962	1,295	1,174	104
1963	1,655	1,447	273
1964	2,092	...	645 planned
1965	2,757	...	665 ,,

* Estimated.

From 1964 to 1970, 25,000 million roubles, about £10,000 million, are to be made available for the construction of new chemical capacity, plus further sums for new processing plants in the plastics industry and for extending raw material and power supplies. The main problems will continue to be the poor state of the chemical equipment industry, technical inexperience in certain sectors, co-ordinating the advance in the oil and chemical industries, and the slowness in converting the results of research into production on an industrial scale. Khrushchev has re-organized the central control over chemicals, but institutional re-organization will not in itself solve his problems. Nevertheless, the chemical industry will continue to grow fast. But it may be reasonably doubted whether more than a few, if any, of the plans will actually be achieved. Overtaking its American counterpart by 1970, except in one or two products, remains an illusion.

BUILDING MATERIALS AND BUILDING

Determined efforts have been made, with Khrushchev's encouragement, to secure significant improvement in Soviet housing conditions.

So bad had they become before he took interest that industrial labour productivity as a whole has been suffering. In 1957, the total space per person, exclusive of the collective farm population, was about 5.5 sq. metres against the British standard of 15.7 to 20 sq. metres and America's 28 sq. metres. Overfulfilment of ambitious housing plans became the keynote, so that, in 1960, 82.8 million sq. metres of urban houses were built against 32.3 million sq. metres in 1955. Under the Seven-Year Plan, the aim was to build some 650 to 660 million sq. metres during the whole period of 1959 to 1965, and, in 1959, urban completions amounted to 80.7 million sq. metres against 71.2 million in 1958, a rate of increase which suggested that, as under the Sixth Five-Year Plan, the new plan would be substantially over-fulfilled. Use of novel methods and materials, notably pre-fabrication and pre-cast concrete parts, were behind the successes of the late 1950s and made it seem as if rapid expansion would continue. In 1960, however, the increase in housing completions was small and there was actually a slight drop in 1961 and little recovery in 1962, when only 81 million sq. metres were completed. In 1963, which was a difficult year for the whole Soviet economy, there was a further drop in completions to 77 million sq. metres and under the new Two-Year Plan (1964-65), which has been brought into operation to overcome the difficulties of rounding off the Seven-Year Plan, it has been confirmed that a significant underfulfilment of the original Seven-Year Plan is now expected. However, despite these setbacks, the USSR built about $2\frac{1}{2}$ times as much urban housing in 1963 as in 1955, though most of it was of pretty poor quality. In the meantime, the output of building materials, such as cement, pre-cast concrete parts and window glass, continued to go up fast. Unfortunately, owing to the size of the housing problem which in the towns is growing rather than diminishing because of the influx of people from the countryside, it is unlikely that by 1965 there will be as much as 6.5 sq. metres of poor quality living space per head of urban dwellers.

LIGHT INDUSTRIES

This is a Soviet classification comprising the textile, clothing and footwear industries. Between them, they account for only 4.5 per cent of the USSR's industrial capital but, in accordance with Khrushchev's promises to improve the supply of consumer goods, investments in this group increased at a slightly higher percentage rate between 1956 and 1960 than the average for industry as a whole, although the reverse was true of 1961. Very much more than is currently being done to improve these industries would be required before they could compare with their western counterparts. The comparison of production figures makes little sense, since it is here that the problems of poor quality, finish and design mean so much more than sheer volume of output. The main Soviet figures are as follows:

SOVIET OUTPUT OF TEXTILES AND CLOTHING

	Unit	1952	1958	1961	1962	1963	1965 Plan
Cotton Fabrics	million sq. m.	3,551	4,308	4,875	4,914	5,069	5,860
Woollen Fabrics	,, ,,	240	385	454	469	471	643
Silk Fabrics*	,, ,,	180	690	683	787	801	1,256
Linen	,, ,,	227	440	493	485	509	581
Hosiery	million pairs	585	888	1,001	1,033	...	1,250
Rubber Footwear	,, ,,	124	159	164	157	...	over 210
Leather Footwear	,, ,,	237	356	443	456	463	515

* Includes artificial and synthetic fabrics.

Production as a whole is expanding and will continue to do so, but the performance of this group of industries has little bearing on Khrushchev's competition with the West.

CHAPTER VIII

Soviet Agriculture, Fishing and Forestry

Much has already been said about the strained and erratic development of agriculture under Communism. Ever since 1928, which marked the initiation of full central control, one of the outstanding features has been the unrealistic nature of agricultural planning. This can best be seen from the official figures of the output of grain, including legumes.[1] Production of 127 million tons in 1950 was planned, compared with the best pre-war output of 91 million tons in 1937. When, after the death of Stalin, the figures were disclosed, output in 1950 was shown to be only 81 million tons. The plan for 1955 was 125 million tons, and the output claimed was still only 107 million tons. These particular failures were due not only to the continued resentment of the rural population at having been deprived of their farms and to the derisory prices offered by the Government for compulsory deliveries of produce, but, until recently, official unwillingness to invest adequately in agriculture.

Khrushchev seriously began his reforms in September 1953, when official prices were considerably improved, better conditions for the free market[2] began to be provided and the conditions for payment in kind by collective farms for the services of the State-owned machinery and tractor stations (MTS) were made less exacting. The following February saw his announcement of the Virgin Lands campaign. This meant increasing the sown area from about 375 million acres by about one-fifth from land to be ploughed up, largely in Kazakhstan, the Volga region and various parts of Siberia. This huge undertaking was tackled with characteristic vigour, mainly by the establishment of huge State-owned farms largely worked by volunteer labour from the old-established agricultural areas and the towns.

---

[1] Legumes, mainly peas and beans for fodder, have not so far been an important item, but they have always been included with grain.

[2] Members of collectives sell the produce of their private plots on this market.

Most of the ploughing was completed in 1956, which was a good year climatically and saw a great jump in grain output, which was claimed to be as much as 128 million tons.

The Sixth Five-Year Plan had by then been announced, with its aim of an output of 180 million tons of grain and legumes by 1960, to be achieved not only by further increases in acreage, but the transfer of much land, mostly in western USSR, to the production of maize from other crops and improved supplies of fertilizers and machinery. Under the right conditions, maize is very productive, but when it does not ripen it is used green as silage and this is given a grain equivalent for inclusion in the total of Soviet grain production. In 1957, weather conditions were poor, and, for all the increased acreage and development of maize, the total grain crop officially claimed fell back to only 105 million tons. But with exceptionally good weather in 1958 and the dividends really beginning to flow markedly from Khrushchev's reforms, the record harvest of 141 million tons was claimed. By this time, however, the Sixth Five-Year Plan had been abandoned, and when, late that autumn, the Seven-Year Plan was published, the grain output proposed for 1965 was to range from 164 to 180 million tons, against the 180 millions previously intended for 1960. This was a big scaling down of ambitions, but still represented a stiff programme, calling for a faster rate of growth than had ever been achieved before. Agricultural output as a whole was to grow at an average yearly rate of 7.8 per cent compared with one of 7.1 per cent, as officially claimed, for the years 1954–57, but more likely to have been some 5 to 6 per cent. In the table opposite the main production objectives for 1965, as originally laid down, are shown together with those previously intended for 1960, and what was claimed actually to have been produced in that and in certain other years.

Apart from sugar beet, the 1960 output of which was well above plan, the output of all the other main products in that year was far below the original 1960 plan. Nevertheless, as with grain, the production claimed in 1960 was generally much higher than in the disastrous years before Khrushchev initiated his agricultural reforms. The rise in output of meat, milk and eggs was particularly impressive, causing Khrushchev to boast about overtaking the American levels of consumption per head of such products. Despite the rise in output between 1953 and 1960, the 1965 plans, when looked at in detail, are obviously over-ambitious. Output per agricultural worker is supposed to increase by 100 per cent between 1958 and 1965 on collective farms and by 55 to 60 per cent on State farms. To these ends investments in agriculture as a whole between 1959 and 1960 were to be nearly double those between 1953 and 1958, with considerable further emphasis on mechanization, rural electrification and almost a trebling of the supply of fertilizers. There were also to be improvements in techniques, strains of seed and in the supply of insecticides and pesticides and attention to pedigree stock raising. Such promises have been made many times before, and that they were beyond realization can be seen as much in the investment allocations as in the high 1965 output objectives themselves.

SOVIET AGRICULTURAL OUTPUT AND PLANS

Item	Unit	1953 Claim	1955 Claim	1958 Claim	Old 1960 Plan	1960 Claim	1965 Plan
Grain and Legumes	Million tons	82	107	141	180	133	164/180§
Potatoes	,, ,,	...	72	87	157	84	147
Sugar Beet*	,, ,,	...	31	54	47.7	57	76/84
Raw Cotton	,, ,,	3.7	3.9	4.4	6.2	4.4	5.7/6.1
Meat†	,, ,,	2.0	6.3	7.7	12.6	8.7	16.1
Milk	,, ,,	...	44.5	58.8	86.8	61.5	105
Eggs	Thousand million	...	18.5	23.0	46.2	26.4	37.0
Raw Wool‡	Thousand tons	...	256	322	466	355	548

* Factory processed.
† Including lard and offal.
‡ Greasy weight.
§ Raised to 192 millions in 1961 to allow for production of greatly increased amounts of pulses.

According to the Seven-Year Plan, State agriculture was to have productive investments between 1959 and 1965 of 15,000 million roubles, whereas the collective farms to which the machinery and tractor stations and most of their equipment had largely been transferred, were to have total investments of 34,500 millions.[1] At the beginning of the plan the collectives accounted for well over twice as much agricultural land and seven times as many workers as the State farms. They could hardly be expected, therefore, to increase their labour productivity much faster than State farms. In addition, the collectives were supposed to find this capital out of their own profits—a pious hope. Comparison of the proposed investments of agriculture with those of industry brings out the preference enjoyed by the latter. The total of 49,500 million new roubles proposed for

[1] Total investments are officially defined as including such items as social amenity buildings.

agriculture looks small in comparison with the 113,900 millions allocated to the extractive and manufacturing industries which, in 1958, were employing about half as many workers as in agriculture. Their productivity was to rise by 50 per cent per worker, whereas agricultural workers were supposed with their much smaller allocation to increase their productivity by around 95 per cent. It is wrong, however, to labour this disparity between the total value of agricultural and industrial investment because of the great dissimilarities between the two industries, particularly the attitude of mind of the people involved. Such is the lack of interest of the average Soviet farm worker in anything but his private plot that nothing like full use is made of the investments made. But it can legitimately be pointed out that, in industry, with its favoured treatment so far as investment is concerned, and the generally greater identity of interests of workers and planners, productivity plans are nevertheless always underfulfilled. And, before the Seven-Year Plan went into operation, it could be confidently forecast that the much more ambitious productivity plans for agricultural workers would, as before, turn out to be politicians' dreams. Use of the United States analogy is profitable. In terms of grain, the USSR is supposed, in 1965, to produce about as much as was produced in 1958 by the USA, where both soil and climate are far more favourable. To do this, Soviet agriculture has been promised an average of 29 kg. of fertilizer (nutrient value) per hectate of arable land compared with over 40 kg. at present in the USA, where it is still increasing. Nor will the amount of machinery likely to be available approach that available in the USA. The promise is for a tractor park of 1,700,000 or about one-third of that of the USA. Thus, if the tractor plan is fulfilled, output in 1965 is to be 440,000 units, whereas the USA was producing as many as 550,000 in 1960. In the same year she produced 305,000 harvesters against the USSR's planned output for 1965 of around 200,000.[1] Moreover, there is the problem of transport. Failure to cope adequately with this, as well as with that of storage, led to heavy losses in the early days of the Virgin Lands programme. The average Soviet farm covers much larger areas than does the American, yet, with Soviet output of lorries and buses only to reach 550,000 a year by 1965 compared with America's current output of double that number, and the USSR allocating a high proportion to the armed forces, how can Soviet farmers hope to compete with America's?

[1] Only the plan for ordinary grain combines is known. This is 138,200. Generous allowance has been made for maize, potato and beet combines for which the plan has not been disclosed.

The first four years of the Seven-Year Plan for agriculture have done nothing to refute the view that it is utterly unrealistic. Whereas agricultural output as a whole is supposed to increase at a yearly percentage rate of 7.8, even the official index lays claim to nothing better than increases of 0.5 per cent in 1959, 2.2 per cent in 1960, 2.7 per cent in 1961 and 1.3 per cent in 1962. One Soviet spokesman has, in fact, made statements which suggest that output in 1963 fell by 9 per cent. The grain harvest was comparatively poor in 1959 and, although conditions were better in 1960 and 1961, the record output was not surpassed until 1962. In 1963 the hard winter and summer drought caused a severe setback and the USSR was compelled to buy wheat from the West. The output of the main products claimed during the first five years of the Seven-Year Plan has been as follows:

SOVIET AGRICULTURAL OUTPUT UNDER THE SEVEN-YEAR PLAN

Item	Unit	1958	1959	1960	1961	1962	1963	1965 Plan
Grain and Legumes	Million tons	141	126	134	137.3	148.2		164/180*
Potatoes	„	87	87	84	84	70		147
Sugar Beet	„	54	44	58	51	47		76/84
„ „ for fodder	„	...	1.7	5.9	13.3	24.4		
Raw Cotton	„	4.4	4.7	4.4	4.5	4.3		5.7/6.1
Meat	„	7.7	8.9	8.7	8.7	9.5		16.1
Milk	„	58.8	61.7	61.5	62.6	63.9		105
Eggs	Thousand million	23.0	25.6	27.4	29.0	30.2		37.0
Raw Wool	Thousand tons	322	355	355	366	374		548

* Raised to 192 millions because of intended production of greatly increased amounts of pulses.

Instead of the rapid march forward of the late 1950s being accelerated in the early 1960s, the experience throughout agriculture, as revealed by the above figures, has been that of little more than a holding operation. The good harvest in 1958 made possible a substantial increase in the output of meat, eggs and dairy produce in 1959. In 1963 the poor harvest has necessitated a 13 per cent reduction in the herds, pigs suffering most, even though about 13 million tons of the grain deficiency is being met by imports from western countries. Livestock production will fall in 1964 but may rise again a little in 1965 if the next harvest is good. As was to be expected, State investments in farming have been well above the planned level,

F

though those of the collectives have been well below it. In the years 1959 to 1962, the development has been as follows:

FARM INVESTMENTS (PRODUCTIVE)

	1958	1959	1960	1961	1962	1959/65 Planned Annual Average
			Million Roubles			
Collectives	2,462	3,050	2,721	2,739	2,965	4,300*
State Farms	2,279	2,021	2,471	2,984	3,450	2,143
Total	**4,741**	**5,071**	**5,192**	**5,723**	**6,415**	**7,072**

* Estimated from Plan for total investments in collectives.

Owing to considerable transfers of collective farms into the State-owned category, these figures are somewhat misleading on the performances of the two categories, with the State farms apparently investing rather better in relation to plan and the collectives rather worse. It is not remarkable that the record of investment by collective farms has been so poor. For decades this sector of agriculture has been exploited by the Government, and even though it is claimed that, through various concessions, collective farm incomes rose from 5,000 million roubles in 1953 to 13,600 millions in 1961, the resources left over for investment have been minimal. Thus, as recently as June 1962, it was disclosed that despite increases in the State procurement prices for livestock products they were still so low that most farms were incapable of covering production costs. To relieve the critical meat supply situation by providing money incentives for production, procurement prices were raised for meat and butter, but so were the retail prices. This meant that the urban consumer was paying for the concession to agriculture. The government stated quite explicitly that additional central funds could not be diverted from other sectors.

The years 1961 and 1962 saw the wholesale reconstruction of farm administration, further financial relief for the collective farms, and measures for speeding up the supply of machinery, fertilizers and electrification and irrigation. At the 22nd Communist Party Congress in October 1961 the continuing anxiety of the Soviet leaders over the unsatisfactory state of agriculture was also manifest. Little reference was made to the problem of fulfilling the 1965 Plan, attention being diverted to the brilliant prospects for 1970 when, it was said, agricultural output was to be two-and-a-half times as great as in 1960, and for 1980, when the increase was to be three-and-a-half times. Khrushchev then proposed to rely much more heavily than hitherto on peas, fodder beans and other legumes by raising the ratio under these crops from 3 per cent to 20 per cent or more of an expanded grain acreage. The aim was to solve the fodder problem by supplementing maize in the harsher north and east at the expense of oats, bare fallow and sown grasses. Such a programme had many dangers, for there was little experience upon which to build. Peas and beans require more attention than grass, are more prone to disease and, being particularly dirty, are bound to encourage far more weeds than clean fallow. For these reasons, coupled with a shortage of seed, only 9 per cent of the grain-sown area had been put under legumes by 1963.

Another innovation was the 200 h.p. tractor, which, after three years, is still having teething troubles. It is to be used to speed up work in the virgin lands where labour is still scarce and operations must be carried out rapidly because of the short seasons when weather conditions are favourable.

Agriculture's poor performance in 1963 highlighted its drag on the economy and forced Khrushchev to modify many of the policies on which he set such store. Grain farming, with Soviet methods on virgin lands subject to drought, has proved unreliable and costly in lost soil fertility and resources employed. Maize pushed beyond its limits into cold and dry regions has not returned the yield expected of it. The ploughing up of the grasslands and the drastic reductions of fallow have reduced soil fertility and increased soil erosion and weed infestation. Instead of extending the sown area by bringing marginal land under the plough the aim now is to intensify farming in the western and southern areas favoured by climate by applying more fertilizers. Greatly increased efforts and resources are being devoted to secure fulfilment of plans for fertilizer production and allocations have been modified. It is hoped thereby to raise yields to the levels now being obtained in the Netherlands, Denmark and Britain.

For these to be even remotely approached, however, the present excessive waste will have to be eliminated. Workers will have to learn how to use fertilizers, and there must be more and better storage and handling facilities and machines for applying the fertilizer.

Irrigation is to be expanded in association with the increased use of fertilizers, although less urgently because of a number of complex problems. Maize is henceforth to be confined to areas suitable for it or where no other crop would do better. New varieties of wheat are now in favour. Clean fallow, recently so harshly condemned, is now advocated again for virgin lands at least. Collective farms are to be given special credits, enabling them to pay the experts they need, but in general the important problem in Soviet agriculture of providing adequate incentives has still to be solved.

The official Soviet index of agricultural output can be used to expose the crass stupidity of the planners' optimism, despite its double counting and the suspicion that it deliberately puts a favourable gloss on the picture. The relevant figures are as follows:

GROSS AGRICULTURAL OUTPUT OF THE USSR

				Index 1913=100	Yearly Increase Per Cent
1950	..	..	..	140	—
1955	..	..	..	170	3.9
1958	..	..	..	218	8.6
1959	..	..	..	219	0.5
1960	..	..	..	224	2.3
1961	..	..	..	230	2.7
1962	..	..	..	233	1.3
1963	..	..	..	213	−8.6
1970 Plan	..	..		560	14.8

The influence of Khrushchev's initial measures is seen in an increase in the average yearly increase in production from 3.9 per cent between 1950 and 1955 to 8.6 per cent between then and the good year 1958. Under the Seven-Year Plan, the annual increments have shrunk again to well below those between 1950 and 1955, and in 1963 there was a sharp drop. Yet we are asked to believe that between now and 1970 the increment will expand to nearly 15 per cent a year. It will take a lot more than fertilizers, changes in the cropping pattern, and the other promises even to regain the expansion rates of the middle 1950s. However, Soviet agricultural output will rise and, with the normal variations of the weather, will do so faster in some years than it has done since 1958, but the way is still hard. The claim to be rapidly overtaking the economy of the USA is thus seen to be most unconvincing when Soviet agriculture is given anything more than the most uncritical consideration.

The Fishing Industry
No discussion of Soviet food and agriculture would be complete without reference to the important fishing industry. Before the First World War the emphasis had been on shore and inland fishing, but, under Communism, progress was made in deep-sea and mechanized

fishing, although this suffered a severe setback in the Second World War. There was quickened expansion thereafter, based partly on domestic ship construction and on large-scale imports of modern vessels. By 1958, the USSR owned several thousand ships with a combined tonnage of over a million gross tons, or nearly four times that of Britain. In that year, the USSR's deep-sea catch was over two million tons against Britain's one million tons, but the USSR had a further 831,000 tons of fish from her shores and inland fisheries and 311,000 tons of whales. A good deal of detail, much of it confusing, has been released about the Seven-Year Plan for the fisheries. It would appear that the intention is to increase the fleet by about 70 per cent to over 1.8 million gross tons by 1965. The Soviet fishing fleet is already the largest fleet in the world, but there appears to be no reason why such an increase should not be achieved, together with improvements in the type and horsepower of vessels.

Thousands of small boats and hundreds of medium and large trawlers have been ordered, as well as mother ships and transports; Poland and East Germany are already making important deliveries. The outstanding feature is the programme for fish-factory trawlers, a type of vessel which originated in Britain.

A catch of 4.6 million tons of fish of all kinds from all sources is planned for 1965[1]—an increase of 1.7 million tons over 1958. This increase is to be achieved by the following means:

	Addition to Annual Catch by 1965 Thousand Tons
All new vessels	1,700
125 fish factory trawlers	750
Medium trawlers and seiners	350
Three additional Antarctic whaling expeditions ..	400
Three additional Far East whaling flotillas ..	200

When the plan was first announced it seemed somewhat over-ambitious. But so great has been the growth both of the fishing fleet and of the yearly catch, that it seems likely that the catch planned for 1965 will be achieved. Among the problems involved are the need to go farther and farther to find adequate deep-sea fisheries and the difficulties caused by the over-fishing and industrial pollution of inland waters, which, despite a gradually declining catch, still con-

[1] Revised upwards to five million tons in 1962 following the successes of the first three years.

tribute over a fifth of the total. The USSR's fish catch has developed in recent years as follows:

SOVIET FISH CATCH

	1953	1958	1959	1962	1963	1965 Plan
			(Thousand Tons)			
Deep Sea Fishing ..		1,789	1,940			2,730
Whale Fishing		311	360			900
Inland and Coastal Fishing		831	760			1,010
Total	1,980	2,931	3,060	4,100	4,700	4,640

Fish supplies are important to the USSR to help augment the insufficient animal protein content of the Soviet diet. In 1959, fish provided about a fifth of the protein provided by meat, or one-twelfth of all the animal protein intake, when eggs, milk and cheese are also considered. By 1965, if the meat, egg and dairy produce plans are fulfilled, completion of the fish plan would give the USSR rather a smaller proportion of fish in the national protein intake than in 1959. Since the livestock plan is unlikely to be fulfilled and the progress with the fishing industry is so much more satisfactory, it is probable that fish will, in 1965, account for rather a greater share than was planned or is the case today. The comparative ease with which the fish plans can be achieved, and the defence significance of developing seamanship, monitoring of communications and mine-sweeping possibilities suggests that the USSR will press even further forward with her fishing industry.

Other Aspects of the Food Industry
Relatively few statistical details are available on the Soviet food-processing industries. They are undoubtedly large and growing fast. In 1960, when the USSR's capital assets were revalued, the food industries accounted for just over 9 per cent of all industrial capital, which was more than that of coal-mining, the oil and gas, chemical, wood and paper, textile and clothing or building industries, and almost as much as iron and steel. Moreover, between 1956 and 1960, the yearly rate of investment in the food industry rose from 669 million new roubles to 1,247 millions, or by 86 per cent, although they fell to 1,068 millions in 1961. Only chemicals and iron and steel achieved a faster percentage growth of investment than food. This development was consistent with the development of agriculture, and with the promise to diversify the food supply. Under the Seven-Year Plan, investments of 8,250 million roubles are intended between 1959 and

1965 in the light and food industries combined. These seem likely to be over-fulfilled.

Timber and Forestry

The forests of the USSR are vast and virtually inexhaustible, but because of the difficulties of geography and transport, timber is a considerable problem. Ever since rapid economic expansion became the policy, there have been difficulties in meeting the demands of the building, woodworking, paper and cellulose industries and timber plans have generally gone unfulfilled. As the accessible forests became exhausted, operations have been gradually pushed into the remoter and climatically harsher regions, where the problems of labour supply, accommodation and transport have grown. Output claimed and planned in recent years has been, according to the available official figures, as follows:

TIMBER, PLYWOOD AND PAPER PRODUCTION

	1953	1958	1960	1961	1962	1963	1965 Plan
			(Million Cubic Metres)				
Industrial	179.9	250.9	271.0	260.0*	270*	280*	295–300
Wood Fuel ..	112.2	124.1	128.0	126.0	128*	128*	135–140
Plywood	0.9	1.23	1.35	1.4	1.4*	1.5*	2.1
Paper (million tons)	1.6	2.2	2.4	2.6	2.8	2.9	4.2

* Estimated.

Although the industry was rather more successful in the late 1950s than in earlier years, the 1965 Plan is not ambitious by Soviet standards and output has remained sluggish. It fell in 1961, and although it improved in 1962, was still a little lower than in 1960. Recognizing the danger that, unless special measures were taken, the 1965 Plan would not be fulfilled, a State Committee was set up in 1962 for the timber, cellulose-paper and woodworking industries and forestry to co-ordinate planning and research. Investments, which have grown more slowly than in the rest of the economy—in the timber and paper group by 38 per cent between 1956 and 1961 to 614 million roubles— are to go up faster. New timber ranges are to be opened up in the north-west, the Urals, Siberia and the Far East and housing and amenities for timber workers and their families are to be improved. It was hoped by these means to introduce new logging capacities in the RSFSR, which accounts for 90 per cent of Soviet timber output, in 1962 and 1963 equivalent to 7 per cent and 8.5 per cent respectively of the industrial timber hauled in 1961. Progress so far, though slower than intended, has accounted for an annual increase in output of 4 per cent and such a rate of growth if continued would permit the fulfilment of the Seven-Year Plan. But numerous difficulties remain. Now that little prison or forced labour is available, the authorities must rely mainly on volunteers, who are mostly repelled by the poor working and living conditions which can neither be improved overnight nor made as attractive as in the more temperate and populated regions. Machinery and equipment are scarce and, when available, are badly used because of unskilled handling. Road, railway and port facilities are inadequate and, largely because of this and the other shortcomings, there is a colossal waste. For example, it was announced at the 22nd Party Congress by the Chairman of the Council of Ministers of the RSFSR that out of 300 million cubic metres of timber hauled in 1961 about 100 million cubic metres were lost. This was because of overcutting—timber being left to rot in the forests— and large losses in floating and processing. With demand heavy and growing fast and the system of bonuses for overfulfilment of plans continuing to exert its malign influence, the dangers of further over-exploitation of the more accessible forests are great. The new Committee may do some good, but the outlook is not yet healthy.

CHAPTER IX

The East European Communist Countries

The East European Communist countries present an uneven picture of material wealth. The level of income per head, for instance, is estimated by one East European source to be twice as high in East Germany and Czechoslovakia as in Bulgaria. Poland, Hungary and Roumania occupy an intermediate position, while Albania is the most backward of all. This hierarchy of economic strength has altered little in the years of Communist power. By Communist standards these areas of Europe are relatively well advanced. They account for a mere 10 per cent of total Communist bloc population, but produce more than 25 per cent of bloc industrial output. The general standard of living in the more prosperous, such as Czechoslovakia, is probably higher than in such countries as Greece or Turkey. The contribution they make to the economic might of the Communist world is obviously not negligible, but it is rather for another reason that they deserve some consideration here. As in China and the Asian Communist States, it is there that Communist economic techniques have been most recently and thoroughly applied, and where the various consequences of Soviet development strategy can be observed.

Have the East European countries been a fair test of the Soviet model? In terms of physical condition, some of them certainly qualified as under-developed countries before they were taken over by the Communists. This is true of the Balkan States, where a major part of the population was dependent on a low efficiency agriculture, the industrial base was rudimentary, and the standard of living was primitive. But other countries were by no means backward agrarian areas. The so-called German Democratic Republic had been an integral part of the most industrially developed country in Europe. Czechoslovakia, too, though small, was highly developed with a fairly diversified economy. Industry, based on good, if limited, coking coal deposits, considerable steel-making capacity and a tradition of skilled manpower, was strong in the manufacture of heavy machinery and armaments as well as in light manufacturing. This industry was further developed during the German occupation and suffered little war damage. Czechoslovak agriculture was also in a fairly sound condition. The remaining countries of the area, though less advanced, had, apart from Albania, also achieved a certain measure of industrialization. Their communications were an extension of the Western European system, their professional and skilled workers were trained in the European tradition, their economic ideas came from the West, and their trade links were largely with Western Europe. During the war, their links with Germany were, of course, strengthened to the exclusion of all else, but they benefited to some extent from German investment.

All this should be borne in mind when Communist regimes claim the credit for the post-war economic expansion of Central and Eastern Europe. Soviet control meant a severance of trading links with Western Europe and the ruthless exploitation of the economies until the mid-1950s, ranging from wholesale dismantling and transfer of industrial plants to the USSR, to the purchase of raw materials, such as Polish coal, at ridiculously low prices. Reparations were exacted from East Germany on a large scale and to a lesser extent from Hungary and Roumania. Prisoners-of-war were retained in the USSR as cheap manpower for long periods, and joint stock companies, effectively under Soviet control, were set up in most of these countries to milk them of their resources. The situation has improved considerably since the death of Stalin and little direct exploitation now remains, but the Satellites still have to submit to the Soviet pattern of economic control and the Soviet view of priorities, both of which are very costly, and to the forcible orientation of their economies towards the USSR. This is effected through the use of Soviet blueprints, capital equipment of Soviet design, Soviet standards and techniques, and Soviet raw materials. Moreover, the bulk of the output of industrial equipment is exported to the USSR.

By the end of the 1940s, the Communists were in full control of Eastern Europe, and the whole paraphernalia of the Soviet system was gradually introduced. The means of production were nationalized, the financial and distribution systems put under State control, and the collectivization of agriculture begun. The aim was to recreate the Soviet Union in miniature in each country, and the emphasis was on industrialization. Naturally, the primary sector was heavy industry, with consumer goods and agriculture coming a poor second. As the main means, the rate of capital formation was drastically stepped up until anything from 20 to 30 per cent of the countries' net national product was being devoted to gross fixed investment. On average, roughly half of this was channelled into industry. To give this some perspective it is estimated that the rate of investment was about three or four times the pre-war level. This was not achieved without sacrifice: peasants and workers contributed heavily to construction through the device of high turnover taxation on consumer goods.

Not unnaturally this tremendous concentration of resources on industry stimulated very rapid growth rates. The following table gives the rise in gross industrial output claimed for each of the East European countries:

	Pre-war to 1962	1950 to 1962
Poland	8.9 times	4.1 times
Czechoslovakia	4.6 ,,	3.3 ,,
East Germany	3.6 ,,	3.3 ,,
Hungary	5.0 ,,	3.2 ,,
Roumania	6.6 ,,	4.6 ,,
Bulgaria	15.2 ,,	4.9 ,,
Albania	28.4 ,,	6.8 ,,

The average annual rate of growth for gross industrial output claimed over the last twelve years has varied between 10.2 per cent for Hungary and 17 per cent for Albania. These figures are subject to the same criticism that applies to the Soviet data on gross output,[1] but some support is given by the output statistics of the heavier industrial items.

EUROPEAN SATELLITES: COMMODITY PRODUCTION

	Unit	Best Pre-war Years	1945	1950	1962
Hard Coal	Million tons	96	42	95	149
Brown Coal	,,	162	109	198	375
Electricity	Thousand million kWh	29	17	44	135
Steel	Million tons	7	2	8	24
Cement	,,	6	0.5	8	26

Thus, in 1962, the output of hard coal was over 50 per cent higher than pre-war, and that of brown coal well over double. The output of electricity had risen nearly 4.7 times, and steel over 3.4 times. Yet,

[1] See Appendix I.

bearing in mind the population of these countries, the figures for 1962, impressively though they compare with the pre-war best, tell also of economies which are still not highly industrialized. With few short of 100 million inhabitants, Eastern Europe produced only 149 million tons of hard coal, whereas Britain, with 53 million inhabitants, produced 197 million tons. The combined steel output was rather more than that of Britain, while electricity output continues to be somewhat behind. And, as might be expected from these data, the official figures do not claim industrial employment of more than 11.6 million out of a total labour force of over 48 millions. The plans for 1965 are for a continuation of the pressure to industrialize. If, in due course, they are fulfilled the area will still be among the poorer parts of continental Europe. The combined satellite output of about 30 million tons of crude steel planned for 1965 can only be achieved by working extremely lean ore deposits, heavier and heavier imports of ore principally from the USSR, and more and more costly operation of the limited coking coal deposits. Yet, the output will continue to be far behind that of the countries of the European Economic Community which, with some 173 million inhabitants, produced nearly 73 million tons of crude steel in 1962 as well as an abundance of consumer goods—all without forced savings, political police or other coercive devices.

The basic industries were, of course, the priority branches: metallurgy, heavy engineering, energy supply and building materials have leaped ahead leaving other branches behind. These are the achievements claimed; but what has been the cost? There is little doubt that the Soviet growth formula has produced results, but just as in the Soviet Union itself, the development has been patchy and disruptive. The rapid rise in the output of some basic products masks the neglect of others. Industries such as textiles, footwear and foodstuffs have suffered from lack of investment. Capacity expansion in these fields has been only modest, and the increases in output that did occur have been largely achieved at the expense of run-down and obsolete plant. The combination of small investments in these non-priority industries, increasing exports of the goods they produced without compensating imports, and declining quality of output, all placed great obstacles in the way of maintaining an adequate supply of consumer items for the population. This was one form of distortion. Yet another effect of the industrialization drive was to saddle the East European economies with costly and wasteful projects which they could ill afford. In particular, the highly publicized iron and steel plants planned, lacking as they did a proper raw material base, were economically dubious.

They came in for heavy criticism and were in danger of being abandoned shortly after Stalin's death when opposition to costly investment projects was being voiced throughout the bloc. The plant at Dunaujvaros in Hungary, which has been in constant trouble, and at Nowa Huta in Poland were, for example, denounced as 'white elephants'. Only after the planners modified their grandiose expansion schemes did they become a more economic proposition. Similarly, the great Kosice steel works in Slovakia has only recently been revived after being abandoned completely in 1953; significantly, it is now going to specialize in the production of sheet metal for the consumer industry rather than heavy industrial steel. Others, such as the Calbe iron and steel works, designed to operate on the leanest of ores, and the Lauchhammer and Schwarze Pumpe Works for the production of coke from brown coal, limp on, burdening the East German economy. Even in the heavy engineering industry itself, certain 'disproportions' occurred, such as the shortage of important materials and inability to produce essential parts.

Where there is such tremendous pressure to push up the rate of investment, there is usually a concomitant squeeze on consumption. Eastern Europe in the early 1950s was no exception. In Hungary, Poland, Bulgaria and Roumania real wages fell as the level of investment rose: in Hungary, they fell 15 per cent for workers and employees between 1949 and 1952,[1] and in Poland 12 per cent between 1950 and 1953.[2] There were other causes of popular dissatisfaction. As a result of the continued emphasis on the expansion of heavy industry, the construction of urban housing was neglected and the situation was further aggravated by the large increases in town population caused by industrialization and the failure to repair and maintain existing dwellings. Only in Czechoslovakia is the average living space per person in urban areas at present above the official health standard.[3]

It is hardly surprising that, as in the USSR, agriculture has fared badly. Simultaneously, with the attempt to achieve the advantages of large-scale operations and to secure a better balance between vegetable and livestock products, there has been the perpetual preoccupation with rapid industrialization. Thus, agriculture has had to be used as a major source of investment funds. The forced deliveries

[1] *Hungarian Statistical Yearbook*, 1957.
[2] 'The Polish Economy since 1950', *Economic Bulletin for Europe* (United Nations Economic Commission for Europe).
[3] Nine square metres per person as defined in the housing codes of the USSR and Bulgaria.

of farm produce at prices uneconomic to the producer, which are the main means of taxing agriculture, have seriously discouraged the growth of output. Failure to win the co-operation of the rural population has been the inevitable result. Even when the authorities have tried to introduce sensible measures there has been little or no response because the collective system is hated. There has been a failure even within the context of the plans laid down for agriculture. In fact, although the supply of livestock products is better than before the war, it is still inadequate by Western European standards and no major agricultural production plan in the satellites has ever been fulfilled. Taking the area as a whole, production has only now recovered from a big decline during the war to exceed the level achieved by a notoriously primitive pre-war agriculture by about 8 per cent. This can be contrasted with a rise in Western Europe of some 27 per cent in relation to pre-war output. Within this general framework it seems that only Poland, Roumania, Bulgaria and Albania have made definite progress, leaving the others worse off than before. Nor have the problems of rural over-population been solved, except in East Germany and Czechoslovakia, where they were of least importance before the war and from both of which millions of people have either fled or been deported to West Germany since April 1945. Agricultural labour productivity has virtually stagnated at pre-industrialization levels. As the authorities did not see fit to raise productivity by providing enough capital, there was little alternative to maintaining the existing food supply by keeping peasants on the land. In fact, the record in East Europe hardly bears comparison with the progress of other countries undergoing rapid industrialization. In Italy, for example, the agricultural labour force fell by almost a quarter between 1950 and 1958, but remained practically stable in Bulgaria, Hungary and Poland.

The available pre-war and post-war figures of agricultural output and livestock numbers in Eastern Europe are as follows:

	Pre-war Average	1950	1959	1960	1961	1962
			(Million Tons)			
Grain	43.6	36.0	48.7	48.2	48.0	46.2
Potatoes	64.7	60.9	60.2	64.0	64.0	64.3
Sugar Beet	17.6	20.4	23.3	34.0	30.0	
			(Million Head)			
Horses	7.8	...	6.3	5.9	5.3	
Cattle	25.3	...	24.8	25.6	26.7	
Pigs	26.7	...	36.4	38.6	40.6	
Sheep	26.3	...	29.8	30.5	31.3	

Before the war, Eastern Europe exported appreciable amounts of agricultural produce, notably grain; today it is mostly a net importer of grain. The total population to be fed is only a little higher than it was before the war but an appreciably greater proportion of it is in industry. Thus, food consumption is somewhat better than it was in the 1930s with grain and potatoes being used more for the production of the livestock essential to improved diets rather than being exported. Much of the grain now imported comes from the USSR, which is largely paid in satellite industrial products. But as there is much heavy labour now involved in industry and pre-war living conditions were mostly very poor, there can be small cause for satisfaction among the working population over the improvements in diet so far achieved.

What of the human problems of the farmer under the Communist system? At the beginning of 1960, when half of East German farming was still in private hands, the Communist authorities intensified the campaign for collectivization. They knew better than to use the brutality and bloodshed employed by Stalin in the USSR in the 1930s, but resorted to a form of economic and psychological warfare which made life unbearable for those who had refused to join the collectives. The resistance of the East German farmers, which had until then been more stubborn and successul than in most parts of Eastern Europe, finally collapsed. By the middle of the year, the authorities were able to claim complete collectivization. The price paid was high. Large numbers of farmers left the land and fled to the West, and many of those that remained resorted to passive resistance, or even in some cases to outright sabotage. Ignorant bureaucratic interference in farming added to the picture of agrarian muddle. In 1961, the harvest was the worst for many years, and not solely because of the weather. East Germany, which had claimed to feed its people better than West Germany, was beset with food shortages. By 1962, some goods, including butter, potatoes and meat, were rationed. But for the fact that East Germany is Communism's window to the West, little might have been done to relieve these shortages but, as it was, supplies were provided by the rest of the bloc. Ironically enough, Poland, where collectivization had been virtually abandoned, was among the principal contributors.

These then, in outline, were some of the results of attempting to apply the Soviet model to Eastern Europe. The diminishing supplies and deteriorating quality of consumer goods, the recurring food shortages, the lack of improvement in real wages, and the sheer human strain of industrialization all contributed to the disturbances in East Germany in 1953, and in Poland and Hungary in 1956. In East Germany the degree of popular enthusiasm for 'the building of Communism' was expressed unambiguously—refugees were fleeing to the West at a rate of 230,000 a year. Between the proclamation of the 'German Democratic Republic' in the autumn of 1949 and the humiliating decision to build the Berlin Wall, two and three quarter million people fled to the West—from a country with one of the highest living standards in the bloc.

But in spite of the difficulties imposed by geography and geology, and the unwillingness of the population to accept both Soviet domination and the sacrifices entailed by forced development, some East European industrial statistics make impressive reading. It was not the Soviet technique of growth stimulation alone that produced results. This had to be, and is still, combined with coercive institutions: the State-controlled enterprises, centralized planning and distribution, collectivized agriculture, the powerful administrative pressure through Party and bureaucracy, to say nothing of the secret police. It is questionable whether Soviet economic strategy could be employed in a democratic State. Both the structure of the economy and the nature of its development pre-suppose autocratic political control. The sacrifice of steep investment rates and the deliberate neglect of nearly everything but heavy industry, for instance, are hard to imagine in the more normal context of consumer preferences and free choice of response to market situations among entrepreneurs. All this should be borne in mind when considering the application of Soviet methods to other countries. However, even with a totalitarian Government, there are limits to the pressure that can be applied, as was eventually discovered in Eastern Europe.

Following the death of Stalin, an effort was made to ameliorate some of the worst effects of the precipitate and lopsided industrialization of the East European countries, for Soviet exploitation and the attempt at autarkic development had brought them to the point of ruin. This change was encouraged by the Poznan riots and the Hungarian uprisings of 1956, which, among other things, demonstrated to the authorities the relationship between consumer welfare and popular discontent. The rate of industrial growth was moderated, a larger slice of the national income allocated to consumption, and more investment directed to light industry and agriculture. These reforms varied from country to country. In Poland, where agriculture was of the first importance, collectivization caused so much hindrance to progress that after 1956 it was virtually abandoned. With the resumption of private farming, inhibiting though it is to large-scale operation, output has improved out of all recognition. Nevertheless, the country has still needed to accept surplus grain from the USA. Since the mid-1950s, the standard of living in Eastern Europe has been slowly improving, but measured against the low level of 1953, the improvement is still inadequate. Excluding Czechoslovakia and East Germany, material conditions are worse than in the poorer countries of the West.

The death of Stalin also marked a change in the Soviet attitude, and a moderation of what had become the self-defeating policy of crippling exploitation. Discriminatory trade prices were partly revised, advisers withdrawn and a start made on the dissolution of the notorious Joint Stock Companies. But in spite of the modifications made on satellite economic plans, there were still growing lags between industrial capacity and raw material supplies, so rather than face the prospect of bolstering up their economies indefinitely, the Soviet Union made its first attempt in 1955 to create an intra-satellite economy of mutual dependence. The agency used for this purpose was the Council of Mutual Economic Assistance (CMEA), which had been started in 1949 as a reply to the Marshall Plan but had remained of little significance. This first experiment in co-ordinating planning to eliminate wasteful duplication broke down. The political ferment of 1956 once again gave new urgency to the fulfilment of Soviet designs in Eastern Europe. The immediate task was to restore economic and political order. This took the form of emergency credits, cancellation of outstanding debts and even the payment to Poland of compensation for the USSR's previous purchases of hard coal at far less than world prices. Once a measure of stability had been achieved, the USSR turned again to the problem of the intra-bloc economy. Economic co-ordination is now the focal point of Soviet economic policy in Eastern Europe and the satellites are under constant pressure to abandon some of their individual self-sufficiency for the sake of more international specialization within the bloc. This, however, is unpopular. The various countries are reluctant to abandon departments of industry which they have built up, usually at great cost, and thereby become dependent on someone else who, for all the international 'fraternalism' of Communism, they do not entirely trust. Pressure is also being brought to bear on the satellites to abandon their traditional industrial and technical specifications, which conform largely to those of the rest of the world, for Soviet ones. This approach has been going on for many years but is as unpopular as ever even among the leading Communists because it is troublesome and costly and makes it harder for them to trade with the free world,

G

where they can earn good currency and purchase imports, particularly of advanced technological equipment, not obtainable within the Soviet bloc.

In 1962, partly to counter the growing influence of the European Economic Community and partly to mobilize East Europe against China, the USSR sought to improve the organization of CMEA. This now has a considerable staff in Moscow and meets twice yearly in one or other of the member countries in which are to be found the various permanent commissions specializing on general industrial groups, etc. Khrushchev even suggested that a central planning organ should be created to work out a single development plan for the whole region. The Roumanians, who had plans of their own for heavy industry which did not meet with Soviet approval, resisted this idea. In the summer of 1963, it was further agreed to co-ordinate the various national plans for the period 1964–70. These all envisaged further rapid economic development and paid lip service to the continuation of strong links with the USSR. But difficulties can be expected on the issue of obtaining advanced technological equipment from the West. Poland, Roumania, Hungary and possibly Czechoslovakia are among the satellites which are anxious to do this. Seeing that the USSR itself buys western equipment, it will be difficult for it to oppose these wishes. Lack of foreign exchange may well prove to be the strongest limiting factor.

For the bloc to be properly welded into a single economic whole, the need for CMEA to be equipped with a powerful trade investment bank has long been discussed. What has so far emerged is the International Bank for Economic Co-operation, which began operation on January 1, 1964. It has only two modest functions, the chief of which is to operate a multiple clearing of the member countries' trading accounts. It does not impinge on the economic sovereignty as its decisions have to be unanimous.

The East European countries have been cajoled into making their contribution to the programme for the Communist penetration of Africa, Free Asia and Latin America and providing the USSR and, until recently, China with as much as possible of what they need for the execution of their own plans. Of these two tasks, by far the most important is the second, and this naturally restricts the resources that can be spared for the under-developed world. It is significant that 70 per cent of bloc trade is confined to dealings among themselves. The early aim of creating separate autarkic communities is now superseded by the policy of welding together a co-operative and self-sufficient comity of bloc Powers. For the moment at least, the tactics of trade and aid to the emerging nations are subservient to this major strategy.

In forcing the pace of industrialization the Communists have set themselves a task which they claim would never have been possible under capitalism. This is only partly true. Substantial economic progress would certainly have been achieved in Eastern Europe after the Second World War under non-Communist rule. The great advance of technology throughout the whole industrial world, and the acceptance of the Marshall Plan and the encouragement of economic cooperation among all the countries of Europe, would have seen to that. The output of basic and extractive industries would certainly have grown, though not as fast as under the Communists, and much more attention would have been paid to consumer goods and housing; agriculture would have been encouraged instead of coerced. This is clearly shown by the post-war development of Italy, a country no better endowed with natural resources than the East European countries and which, before the Second World War, did not rank as industrially important. Moreover, like Eastern Europe, she suffered German occupation and had been fought over from end to end. Italian output figures comparable to those given for the satellites earlier in this chapter are shown below:

ITALIAN OUTPUT OF CERTAIN BASIC ITEMS

	Unit	In Best Pre-war Year	1945	1962	1962 as Per Cent of Pre-war Italy	E. Europe
Hard Coal	Million tons	2.3	0.7	6.9	300	155
Brown Coal	„	2.1	0.8	1.7	81	231
Electricity	Thousand million kWh	15.5*	12.7	62.7	403	466
Steel	Million tons	2.3	0.4	9.5	413	342
Cement	„	4.6*	...	20.2	439	433

* 1938.

In basic production the post-war Italian achievement compares well with Eastern Europe. The general rise in Italian industrial production since 1938 has been threefold: even using the suspect East European data, this is equivalent to the advance claimed for East Germany. In the twelve years 1950 to 1962, Italian industrial growth has roughly kept pace with the rates claimed not only for East Germany but for Hungary and Czechoslovakia as well. The development of the Italian economy, furthermore, has not been one-sided as in Eastern Europe. While agricultural output in Eastern Europe in 1961 is estimated to have been little more than 8 per cent above the pre-war level, Italian agricultural production stood at 70 per cent above the 1938 level. Italy, moreover, enjoys a high reputation in Western Europe for her output of consumer goods, including such luxuries as motor cars and *haute couture*.

Soviet growth techniques have undoubtedly generated rapid industrial development in the East European satellites, but this can be matched in non-Communist countries such as Italy, where the growth of the whole economy has been much more balanced. Other important non-Communist countries, including all the other members of the European Economic Community, have also achieved rapid industrial growth. For example, France and Federal Germany show gains of 50 and 55 per cent respectively between 1955 and 1962. The industrial output of Japan—a good example of a country to have been American rather than Soviet occupied—rose by 291 per cent between 1955 and 1962.[1]

Although the industrial growth of the bloc has been large, agriculture in virtually all these countries has stagnated or nearly so, giving rise to a profoundly discontented rural population. The consumer goods industries and housing have generally been neglected. The East European economies as a whole are more of a warning that Communism is not the whole answer to man's problems rather than an inspiring example.

[1] See the *Monthly Statistical Bulletin* of the United Nations.

CHAPTER X

The Economy of China

In many ways the economic problems which faced the Chinese Communists in 1949 were similar to those which faced the Soviet Communists thirty years earlier, but were probably much greater. Both had vast territories and populations whose livelihood was largely dependent on a primitive agriculture. Both had ample, mostly untapped, natural resources, with the USSR appreciably better endowed than China with minerals, arable land and forests. The USSR inherited a good deal more industrial capacity, both material and human, than did Communist China and had at its disposal the remains of a much more developed administrative machine. The initial problems of the two regimes were, however, much the same—a legacy of corruption, currency inflation, war weariness and chaos, and the attendant fear of civil war and foreign intervention. What China needed was good government to enable her to recover from thirteen years of warfare and over a century of humiliating foreign intervention in her affairs, during which economic progress had been extremely slow. Had it been obtainable, foreign aid on a scale comparable with that received by the Nationalists both from UNRRA and direct from the USA, but largely wasted through incompetence and corruption, might have been put to good use; but this was out of the question. The only conceivable outside help was what might be provided by the USSR. But at that time it had too many economic problems of its own to be able to render much material aid to China.

Among the Chinese Communist leaders there were, however, men of great ability and determination. They were fired by the example of Soviet achievements and were willing to learn from the experience of the USSR. Moreover, they had had some experience in administration, first in Kiangsi, part of which they had controlled from 1927 to 1934, and later in Shensi, from which they were never dislodged. Both territories were rural, but this and their mostly peasant origins gave the

Chinese Communists insight into agricultural problems which was largely denied to the town-born Soviet Communists. In the days of their early and limited power, the Chinese Communists concentrated on land and taxation reform and the problem of usury. As China was an agricultural country, this practical experience was invaluable, although it did not prevent them from making serious mistakes later.

In the first year or so, the new Government concentrated in the economic sphere on restoring order, and they dealt intelligently and fairly effectively with inflation. Restoration of communications and large-scale State trading, both wholesale and retail, were among the chief means used. Strict economy, particularly in regard to official salaries, high taxation, the forced sale of lands and the linking of wages to prices also played a considerable part. There was general relief among the public not only because inflation—one of their oldest economic problems—was at last being seriously tackled, but because of the resolute suppression of corruption and banditry. While some of the more glowing western accounts of the popularity of the new regime in the early 1950s need revision, there can be little doubt that it did enjoy widespread acquiescence and support, much as did Italian Fascism and German National Socialism in the early years of their power. This was an important asset to the Communists, since it involved willingness to accept the material sacrifices essential to the creation of economic stability. Not even the serious difficulties caused by droughts and floods in 1949 and later, and the burden of the Korean War could prevent the economy from progressing towards a degree of health unknown for years.

Wedded as they were to Soviet economic ideas, it was only a matter of time before the Chinese Communists would try to establish an economic system similar to that of the USSR, with its collectivized agriculture, State-owned industries, a high rate of accumulation based on indirect taxation, great emphasis on investments in basic and heavy industry and long-term central economic planning. They began to experiment with a rudimentary form of planning in 1950 with the issue of yearly objectives for the output of certain industries. Late in 1952, it was announced that the first Five-Year Plan would begin in 1953, less than four years after the advent of Communist control. This was extremely ambitious, since China had neither the administrative nor the statistical system essential to thoroughgoing Soviet-type planning. Agriculture had not been collectivized, much of such modern industry as existed was still privately owned, as was a great part of trade. If central planning was to be effective it had to secure the co-operation of China's many thousands of small enterprises, most of whose owners had not a Socialist outlook.

It is hardly surprising that the production targets for 1957 were not made known until the summer of 1955, although the principles underlying the plan were published in September 1953. These made it quite clear that the capital goods industries were to grow faster than those making consumer goods; that agriculture was to be the handmaid of industry by providing grain for the feeding of the industrial population, raw materials and surpluses out of which industrialization could be financed; and that labour productivity was expected to rise faster than wages in the interest of capital accumulation. For the Chinese, most of whom were living at little better than a subsistence level, such principles were ominous, but much depended on the pace demanded. It turned out to be rapid. Industrial output was to be doubled, nearly 60 per cent of investments were to be industrial, and under 8 per cent were to go to agriculture, forestry and water conservation. The subordination of agriculture in this way repeated the Soviet error and was ultimately to lead to serious consequences. Yet it would be unfair to put this preoccupation with rapid industrialization solely down to a doctrinaire approach. By plundering agriculture and the death of millions of peasants through famine and violence the USSR had built up industries without which it would have succumbed to Nazi Germany. The Chinese Communists had obtained power by military means against the will of the world's greatest industrial power. Rightly or wrongly, but understandably, the Chinese Communists felt that the need for industrial strength was urgent.

To secure the implementation of their economic plans, it was necessary for the Government to obtain the co-operation of workers, craftsmen, businessmen, manufacturers and other owners of enterprises as well as the farmers. Severe rules for the operation of private undertakings had been promulgated at the end of 1950 and a year later there was a violent intimidation campaign in which the owners were accused of various kinds of economic 'crimes' and workers were officially encouraged to denounce their employers. Relaxations followed in which Government help was promised in the form of loans and contracts and there were Government-sponsored consultations between the regime and the owners, ostensibly to help the latter to integrate their activities into State plans. But the pressure against the owners was soon resumed. By means of penetration, 'joint under takings' (in which the State assumed a share in private firms), and political and economic pressure, resistance was worn down and virtually all owners of industrial and business concerns were relieved of their property.

There was a corresponding movement in the countryside where, under the Nationalists, there had been a mixture of peasant owner-ship and small tenants, though the average size of Chinese estates was much less than that of the estates in pre-Communist Eastern Europe and Russia. Until shortly after the Communist take-over of the mainland, the emphasis was on 'land reform', under which small tenants and the landless were encouraged by the Communists to seize the estates and, in some areas, the land of the richer peasants. There was much violence and production suffered, so it was not long before the legal status of peasants was legally defined so that the activity of the more efficient (and usually the richer) holders should not be im-paired. But matters were not allowed to rest long at that, for collec-tivization was the ultimate intention. And here it was that the previous experience with administration of agricultural territories probably stood the Communists in good stead. In March 1953, a campaign was launched to convince the peasants that to pool their resources and co-operate among themselves would be economically advantage-ous. Collectivization came, in fact, in four stages. At the start, there were temporary Mutual Aid Groups which worked out at an average size of some ten families who pooled their labour, tools and draught animals, but retained the ownership of their land and confined their co-operation mostly to seed-time and harvesting as, in fact, had widely been done before Communism. Next followed the permanent Mutual Aid Groups, in which individual land ownership was still retained but co-operation was much less restricted. The Agricultural Producers' Co-operatives, which came soon afterwards, were distin-guishable from the Soviet collectives mainly for covering a much smaller average area, which was unavoidable because of the different physical conditions of the two countries, and because in China the payment to members included an allowance for the amount of land contributed as well as for work done. The land was now pooled and worked in common and there were the usual small private lots. Finally, in the full collective, payment to members was based solely on the labour carried out.

In carrying out their agricultural programme the authorities began cautiously, for they were determined to avoid the bloodshed and violence of the Soviet collectivization drive of the early 1930s. Thus, they did not aim at going further than the second stage for more than 35 per cent of the farms by 1957. Much was made officially of the voluntary nature of the process. Participants were legally entitled to withdraw from membership of the various types of co-operative unit which were established. However, such was the power of the party and the influence of its members that nobody could withdraw without incurring frightening consequences or remain outside the currently approved unit for long. So, in the event, what was intended to begin slowly, gained momentum and caution was thrown to the winds. More and more pressure was applied and it was claimed that the whole process was virtually completed in 1956.

There were plenty of Communist enthusiasts to act as collective farm chairmen and local inspectors, to see that instructions were carried out and that work was properly done; pilfering and black marketeering were kept to a minimum. Not unimportant was the small size of the collective and the comparatively dense population which lent themselves to supervision more of a factory standard than was possible in the much larger collectives of the USSR or Eastern Europe.

Important steps for the industrialization programme were the agreements reached with the USSR between 1950 and 1956 under which China was to be provided with 211 Soviet-designed plants, later amalgamated into 166 projects, to be built by Soviet experts. A further 125 such projects were added under agreements in 1958 and 1959. These included electric power stations, colliery, oilfield and refinery plant, iron and steel, heavy engineering and chemical plants as well as other important installations in the basic and armaments industries. They accounted for the most significant of the 700 new works which were to constitute the main industrialization effort. For example, Soviet-built iron and steel plants accounted for nearly three million tons of the total crude steel output of 5.4 million tons claimed for 1957. But, like the large volume of armaments provided by the USSR to China during and after the Korean War, the Soviet plant and technical aid had to be paid for. They were partly financed by medium-term Soviet credits worth no more than $430 million in all, redeemable in the form of exports of foodstuffs, notably soya beans, and minerals such as tin and tungsten, which were scarce in the USSR. The credits were taken up during the course of the plan, when total imports from the USSR were $3,730 million, including $1,170 million worth of machinery and equipment, those not being covered by the credits being paid for by exports. Many Soviet technicians went to China both to do survey work and build the plants and to help in their initial operation and in the instruction of the Chinese. Chinese students studied in Soviet higher educational institutions and gained experience in Soviet works.

In many respects these transactions were similar to those made in the earlier years of industrialization in the USSR. Long-term loans were not forthcoming, but Western European and American industrialists were prepared to sell plant and provide technicians. The cost was met by the export of Soviet food and raw materials, although the former could as ill be spared by the population as could Chinese food exports to the USSR.

The main production objectives of the ambitious first Chinese Five-Year Plan were claimed to have been exceeded, although many difficulties were experienced; these included shortages of raw materials, transport bottlenecks and a great lack of consumer goods which increased inflationary pressures. The situation was at its worst in 1956, when the authorities permitted a relaxation in the pressure for investments and greater output of consumer goods, the effect of which was felt mainly in 1957. The production of certain key items claimed for 1957 compared with 1952 and in the best pre-Communist year was as follows:

	Unit	Pre-Communist Maximum*	1952	1957 Planned	1957 Claimed
Coal	Million tons	61.9	66.5	113.0	130.0
Crude Oil	,,	0.3	0.4	2.0	1.5
Electricity	Thousand million kWh	6.0	7.3	15.9	19.3
Steel	Million tons	0.9	1.4	4.1	5.4
Cement	,,	2.3	2.9	6.0	6.9
Metal Cutting Machines	Thousands	5.4	13.7		28.0
Cotton Yarn	Million Bales	2.4	3.6	5.0	4.7
Grain	Million tons	150.0	156.9	182.0	185.0
Cotton	Thousand tons	1,032.0	1,304.0	1,635.0	1,640.0

* Including Manchuria.

It was officially claimed that the plan as a whole had been over-fulfilled by 17 per cent, with capital construction work 13 per cent more than planned, although general figures such as these, with all their statistical pitfalls, must be treated with reserve. However, the physical output figures for such important basic items as coal, power, iron and steel and cement were also claimed to be well in excess of plan. Crude oil output was said to have been more than trebled yet, in 1957, it was 25 per cent below plan and still low for a country of China's size and ambitions. This reflected the lack of good or accessible resources, oil being one of China's few serious mineral deficiencies. The rise in iron and steel output was remarkable, for China virtually had no such industry before Communism, the only significant pre-Communist developments having been under Japanese rule in Manchuria, where the works had been looted by the USSR at the end of the war. Subsequent Soviet help in rehabilitating the Manchurian plants and Communist dedication to iron and steel were responsible.

In agriculture, apart from collectivization, the emphasis was on irrigation, the extension of the area sown to grain, and increasing attention to cotton growing.[1] The really suitable land was limited to about 100 million hectares and it had long been intensively cultivated. The extension of the sown area, therefore, meant increased multi-cropping in the old-established farmlands, opening up some of the barren regions of the north (which was done by State farms) and considerable transfers of population from over-populated regions by development of some of the mountainous territories of the west and south-west. The use of better implements and of fertilizers was encouraged but, with China's limited industrial resources and the small allocation of capital to agriculture, little could be done to provide artificial fertilizers or to encourage mechanization. Cotton growing was encouraged by offering good official prices for the crops, although this meant some diversion of land from grain production. The Chinese textile industry became for a time almost independent of imported cotton, but only at the cost of underemployment of mills and rationing of the consumer.

Despite the collectivization drive during the first four years of the plan and serious trouble with flooding in 1956, the Chinese officially claimed to have secured an increase in grain output in each of the five years 1953 to 1957. However, the marked increase claimed between 1954 and 1955 was probably due in part to an improvement in statistical coverage. Livestock numbers were also claimed to have increased. If true, this was in sharp contrast to Soviet experience, in which collectivization had provoked peasant slaughtering of animals to deny them to the collectives. However, apart from pigs and poultry and draft animals, livestock are relatively unimportant in most of China, with her limited fodder supply and grazing facilities. The claims to have been producing about a quarter as much grain again in the latter years of the plan as in the best pre-Communist year was impressive, but it by no means denoted plenty, since the population was probably much greater than it ever had been under Chiang Kai-shek. During the first Five-Year Plan itself, food production grew

[1] The proposals for agriculture in the first Five-Year Plan were amplified in the Twelve-Year Programme for Agricultural Development, 1956–67, published in 1956.

faster than population, but there were signs that, until a much greater allocation of resources could be made to agriculture—in particular, the supply of artificial fertilizers needed to be increased much faster than hitherto—the rate of growth of output could not reasonably be expected to be maintained, and it would soon be outstripped once again by that of population.

Early in the discussions for the second Five-Year Plan, it seemed as if the Chinese authorities recognized the need to give more attention to consumer goods and agriculture, although in the latter case attention was still to be concentrated on the kind of improvement which did not call on scarce resources. Irrigation work was to continue, the use of better seeds was to be encouraged, better implements were to take the place of the many whose design dated back for centuries, and the attack on diseases and pests was to be maintained. Heavy industry was to enjoy priority, as before, and the production aims for 1962 were to include 190 to 210 million tons of coal, 5 to 6 million tons of crude oil, 40 to 43 thousand million kWh of electricity and 10.5 to 12 million tons of crude steel. Despite the modest means to be used, agriculture was expected to produce 240 millions of grain and 2.15 million tons of cotton. All in all, the growth rates envisaged were of about the same order as under the first Five-Year Plan, but before it went into operation the Chinese authorities had begun to throw off all ideas of moderate economic growth. There came instead the twin revolutionary ideas of the Great Leap Forward and of the Communes.

The Great Leap Forward was intended to secure such a spurt in productivity as would put in the shade any growth previously achieved under either capitalism or Communism. The Communes involved sudden and far-reaching changes in the whole pattern of living and, although launched somewhat later, were to be one of the chief means of securing the Great Leap Forward. Before criticizing the folly of those responsible for these fantastic and, as they were soon to prove, disastrous programmes, it is appropriate to reiterate the economic predicament in which they felt their country to be as a world power. The first Five-Year Plan, despite its successes, had done no more than set China at the beginning of the very long road she needed to travel before she could seriously hope to compete with the industrial might of the other world Powers. In 1957, for all her record output of coal, electricity and steel, the amount of these per head of population was tiny. Compared with the USA, Britain, the USSR and Japan, this was as shown in the table opposite.

The USA, whom China feared the most, had 147 times as much

electricity output per head and 74 times as much steel per head as China. Japan, her old enemy, after an impressive post-war recovery, had three times as much coal, 30 times as much electricity and nearly 18 times as much steel per head. China, whether she saw herself in the van of Communist expansion in Asia or threatened by the American presence in Formosa, South Korea and Japan, was unable to resist the temptation to try to reduce faster than was humanly possible the disparity between her own industrial development and that of the great Powers. Awareness of the huge size of this disparity must have been as important a consideration as the confidence bred by the successful aspects of the first Five-Year Plan. Add to these the ignorance of industrial and economic problems and there are probably the main ingredients of the fateful decisions which led to the Great Leap Forward and the Communes.

OUTPUT PER HEAD OF POPULATION IN 1957

				Coal Tons	Electricity kWh	Crude Steel Kilogrammes
USA	..	..	..	2.725	4,409	596
UK	..	..	..	4.451	1,782	413
USSR	..	..	..	2.260	1,023	250
Japan	..	..	..	0.584	900	139
China	..	..	..	0.193	30	8

The campaign for the Great Leap Forward, which was to take place in the three years 1958 to 1960, was officially launched at the National People's Congress in February 1958. Gross industrial output during that year was to rise by 14.6 per cent, while that of coal, electricity and steel was to increase by 17, 18 and 19 per cent respectively. It was at this time that China was talking of overtaking the British output of basic industrial products within fifteen years. Thus, allowing for growth in Britain, steel output in China was to rise to 40 million tons by 1972. During ensuing months, the usual Communist hullabaloo was created and workers everywhere were said to be undertaking to increase their output at phenomenal rates and demanding far more ambitious objectives than had been announced in the winter. Many local authorities, recently given increased economic responsibilities, were undertaking to secure the production in 1958 of as much as might have been expected of them in 1967 at the end of the third Five-Year Plan. Remembering that these authorities comprised the party zealots, it is clear that it was here that the 'demands' of the workers for stiffer tasks in 1958 originated. No longer was gross industrial output to rise by a mere 14.6 per cent;

nothing less than a 33 per cent increase was now foreseen, and the year's steel output was to rise to 10.7 million tons instead of the 6.2 million tons envisaged when the Great Leap Forward was first announced.

The basic principle behind this hastily improvised campaign was the mobilization of the efforts of millions of workers outside the main industries so as to superimpose their production on that expected within the original framework of the second Five-Year Plan, such as it was. Rural authorities were ordered to encourage small-scale industrial activity so that within a year or so its output would be equal to that of agriculture. Huge numbers of small undertakings, including mines, were to be started or existing ones extended both by these authorities and the collective farms, helped by designs provided by central government departments and State enterprises, who were also to co-operate with training and advice. This was 'do it yourself' on the grand scale, trying to take advantage of the long slack periods in agriculture and to mobilize women not already employed outside their homes. At virtually no capital cost to the central authorities, it was hoped that the rural population would provide such items as coal, fertilizers, iron and steel of a kind adequate for the simpler types of implements and equipment and, indeed, many finished products themselves; the quickly developing modern undertakings could then concentrate on the more complex items. 'Backyard' blast furnaces with individual capacities of no more than 500 tons of pig iron a year, against the 3,000 tons a day of the world's largest units, seemed to spring up overnight. Such small capacity suggests the charcoal furnaces of antiquity, but China lacked the timber for the necessary fuel and, as illustrations in the Chinese Press have shown, many were tiny copies of modern coke-consuming furnaces.

The commune movement was said to have started in Honan in April 1958, and to have spread rapidly elsewhere, being first announced on Peking radio in August 1958. As summarized by Hughes and Luard[1] 'it took the form of the merging of about 20 or 30 co-operatives including 20,000 or more members, spread over 40 to 100 villages, into single communes, independent administrative and economic units, having control of all the means of production and the entire labour force within its area'.

It 'was said to provide "unified management" of industry, agriculture, commerce, education, and military affairs. Payment of all members, both industrial and agricultural, was partly by wage pay-

[1] 'The Economic Development of Communist China' (Royal Institute of International Affairs and OUP).

ments and partly by the system of "free supply", under which members obtained some of their food, housing, clothing, and other necessaries without payment.[1] Communal dining-rooms and nurseries were widely set up.' The communes saw the abolition of the collective farmer's private plot, something dreamed of by the Soviet Communists and frequently mentioned by them as the ultimate ideal, but which they have not yet dared to put into effect for fear of the reactions it would cause among the rural population. The logic behind this move by the Chinese Communists was impeccable, in that it would put into their hands the control of the whole rural economy —consumption as well as production—and, in theory at least, compel the entire population to conform with the party's plans. Similarly, the other encroachments on some of the last preserves of the private lives of individuals—the crêches and communal dining-rooms—were geared to the complete mobilization of manpower, particularly the women. The whole movement was served up as the greatest advance ever achieved in putting Communist ideology into effect, but the real motive was economic.

The communes did not meet with Khrushchev's approval, who may have been jealous of his Chinese colleagues for their apparent success in achieving what had so far proved beyond the capacity of Soviet Communism, or who was aware of the difficulties involved, and then became a bone of contention between the Soviet and Chinese Communists along with the other issues which have since divided the two parties, and had serious repercussions on China, not least on her economy.

By the end of 1958, it began to be realized that the situation was getting out of hand, though it was claimed that results had exceeded expectations, with the output of grain and raw cotton doubled, a rise of as much as 65 per cent in gross industrial output, a doubling of the output of coal and steel, rises of 50 and 40 per cent respectively in oil and electricity, and a trebling of the production of metal-cutting machine tools. In Peking, the planning authorities no longer had much idea what was being invested or produced or how resources were being used. It was resolved in December to put a brake on the over-rapid development of the communes, to reassure members about their property rights, to ensure that they were not overworked and thus reduce their opposition to the system. The 'military' approach was to be soft-pedalled, planning was to be more careful and realistic and the communes were to concentrate more on

[1] The free supply system lasted only few a months before proving unworkable.

subsidiary and repair work in the interest of agricultural development than on making themselves economically self-sufficient. Early in 1959, inspection teams were sent into the country to see that this resolution was properly observed; by that time it was too late to take measures which could be of much immediate effect.

The year 1959 was one of mounting disillusionment and criticism both within the Communist party and among non-members. There had been colossal waste, confusion and delays in transport and the poor quality of production was beginning to become apparent. The output of the backyard iron and steel plants was found to be almost entirely useless. And, worse than this, there were increasing food shortages. The official myth of almost unqualified success could not be maintained. In August 1959 the authorities were forced to admit that output had not been as great as previously claimed. The 1958 harvest was written down from 375 million tons of grain to 250 million. Even the revised figure was unbelievable, since it was still 35 per cent above the record harvest of 1957 and therefore inconsistent with the current food shortages. Of the claimed total output of some 11 million tons of steel, the three million contributed by the backyard works were eliminated from the official statistics, and the output planned for 1959 was reduced from 18 million to 12 million tons. Although the coal output claimed for 1958 was not written down, the 1959 plan was lowered from 380 to 335 million tons. Both the new coal and steel plans for 1959 were subsequently claimed to have been over-fulfilled—something which still put a strain on credulity, particularly the alleged output of 347.8 million tons of coal, which was inconsistent with some of the available data on coal consumption. The time was rapidly approaching for a complete blackout on economic statistics, the sure sign in totalitarian countries that things are seriously wrong in the economy. In the case of China, the whole statistical system had also run into a hopeless state of confusion.

Worst of all, 1959 was the first of three years in which there were greater than average economic difficulties due both to prolonged droughts in huge areas as well as to great floods. The disasters did not stop the authorities from claiming a grain harvest of as much as 270 million tons which, if it could have been believed, was yet another record, but 1959 was the last full year of Chinese statistical reporting for the time being—on agriculture as well as on industry. However, the Great Leap Forward was not done with yet and, despite the disillusionment of 1959, the pressure was maintained for much of 1960—its final year. Indeed, at the National Peoples' Congress in

March 1960, Li Fu-Chun actually spoke of continuing the Great Leap throughout the 1960s and called for the rapid extension of the communes into the urban areas. The principle of the urban commune was largely the same as that of the rural—to mobilize surplus, largely female, labour to get work done which could not otherwise have been contemplated. The urban commune was to perform such functions as producing materials for the big industrial plants and making consumer goods, which were increasingly scarce as a result of the growing emphasis on basic and heavy industry. There had been some experiment with urban communes in 1958 and 1959, but it was not until after the 1960 Congress that a campaign comparable with that of the rural communes was launched. It was short-lived.

The final stages of disillusionment probably began with the mounting evidence that the 1960 harvest, which was needed to be good, would be worse even than that of 1959. The harm caused by natural calamities was not confined to agriculture; mines in the north-east were flooded, and even some of the big metallurgical plants were temporarily put out of operation. Moreover, the quarrel between the Chinese and the Soviet Communists now reached such a pitch that in July 1960 the Soviet Government ordered the withdrawal of the experts, later said by the Chinese to number 1,380, who were helping in the construction and initial operation of the new industrial and other economic undertakings. Numerous projects had to be cancelled outright for lack of technical advice, and progress at many others was greatly retarded.

The impact on the ordinary people of this combination of misfortunes must have been enormous for, within a matter of half a dozen years, what was traditionally the most conservative and the most numerous class of the population had been subject to a bewildering succession of social and administrative changes depriving them of much of what they had lived for. In return they were given harder and harder work and less and less say in their own destinies. The reaction was bound to be great.

In the summer of 1960, it was officially announced that the main emphasis was to be switched from heavy industry to agriculture. Manpower that had been transferred to local industry was to be returned to the farms and a campaign was launched for capital goods industries to produce agricultural equipment and supplies instead of equipment for other industries. In so far as the latter programme was practicable it was reasonable, for the future of China's industrial development depended heavily on the soundness of agriculture. It has been officially admitted that over half the revenue of the national

H

budget was derived directly or indirectly from agriculture, the budget being the largest single source of industrial investment finance, while agriculture provided over one-third of industrial raw materials and financed about 70 per cent of imports, most of which were for the industrialization programme. Quite clearly, the milch cow had been seriously maltreated. Thus, even the 1960 budget, which saw an improvement in the allocation of investments in agriculture, provided it with no more than 12 per cent of the total. The economic report for 1960 was extremely sketchy, but it admitted that the plan for agriculture as well as those for most of the light industries had not been fulfilled. For heavy industry, the claim continued to be one of over-fulfilment, with steel output said to have reached 18.45 million tons —the only output figure released for the whole economy, and a most improbable one at that.

At the meeting of the Central Committee of the Communist Party in January 1961 it was announced that the level of investment in heavy industry would have to be greatly reduced, and that the emphasis would be less on increasing production and more on improving the quality and variety of output. For a Communist country to take such steps was almost unprecedented, though it was no more than an acceptance of the inevitable. Production had begun to fall sharply. The effects of the general mismanagement of the Great Leap Forward were being felt and food shortages affected productivity in the labour intensive industries. More and more factories were forced to close, or operate below capacity by raw material shortages.

At the same time as general retrenchment was taking place, the commune movement steadily receded. Nothing further was heard of urban communes while, in the countryside, by 1959, their economic responsibilities had been transferred back to 'production brigades', which roughly corresponded to the former co-operatives. The reversion did not stop there. In the course of the next two years the responsibility for framing local production plans and remunerating the peasants was assumed by the production teams, which more or less correspond to the former mutual aid groups. In many cases, ownership of land, animals and tools, and the day-to-day tasks of organizing farm production were handed over to still smaller working groups. At the same time, new encouragement was given to side-line occupations and the cultivation of private plots; and so-called free markets were restored, to handle the resulting output and to meet the resurgence of black marketeering and corruption. The authorities soon recognized that the centralized controls of the communes were unable to cope with local problems and emergencies in the diverse agriculture of China. What was even more significant, they had reverted to a pattern of agricultural organization typical of the much earlier stages of collectivization. This must have been humiliating for the Chinese after all their boasts about the ideological superiority of the communes. That they regarded it essentially as an emergency means of stimulating agricultural production was to be made clear by subsequent moves to curtail some of the freedoms that had been granted in the countryside. The food shortages remained acute in 1961, but in 1962 the measures taken began to pay off; although the grain harvest was little better than in the previous year, vegetables and other items produced by individual peasant initiative began to be more plentiful.

The impact of the serious economic situation on China's foreign trade was immediate and striking. Up to 1961, imports of foodstuffs had been negligible, but now China suddenly became a considerable purchaser on the world grain market. During the year she bought about six million tons of grain, mostly from Canada and Australia, at a cost of about £130 million, or about 40 per cent of her total imports from the West. Credit terms made it possible to defer about a third of this bill to 1962, but, with agricultural exports much reduced, imports of capital goods from the non-Communist world had to be severely cut. Such imports were kept to a minimum in 1962–63, for in each year China was obliged to spend well over £100 million on imports of grain. The effect of the internal difficulties on China's trade with the bloc was also great, though an equally important explanation for its decline lay in the abrupt ending of the Soviet technical assistance programme in 1960. In the previous decade, Chinese imports from the USSR, consisting mainly of machinery and equipment, oil and industrial raw materials, had risen from £140 million in 1950 to a peak of £340 million in 1959. In 1961, they fell sharply to £130 million, and in 1962 were a mere £85 million. In the latter year China was still obtaining essential oil products and spare parts and replacements for her existing stock of Soviet equipment, but imports of new plant had virtually ceased. This was in large part due to the scaling-down of China's industrial plans, but it also stemmed from her determination to clear all remaining debts to the USSR as quickly as possible. Although exports of foodstuffs and agricultural raw materials fell to negligible proportions in 1961 and 1962, China still achieved export surpluses in those years, thanks to her ability to maintain exports of textiles and other consumer goods at much the same level as before. By the end of 1962 the debt outstanding was probably under £200 million, and the Chinese have said that they intend to repay this by 1965 at the latest. Trade with the countries of Eastern Europe has likewise fallen greatly.

No official statistics for 1961–62 were released, but there are reasons to believe that industrial output fell by between a third and a half below 1959 peak levels. Considerable idle capacity existed in iron and steel, power and most other basic industries largely as a result of the continuing acute shortages of fuel and raw materials. Industries serving agriculture, particularly the chemical fertilizer sector, were, in contrast, short of capacity, but investment resources for their expansion were not available. Labour productivity fell and the frenzied excitement of the Great Leap Forward was replaced by a general air of apathy.

There was considerable urban unemployment despite measures to return people to the countryside. These moves were officially presented as a means of providing more rural labour, but were unpopular both with townsfolk who faced the prospect of an even worse food situation in the country, and with the peasants who did not need the help of the returnees. This situation undoubtedly contributed to the exodus of Chinese to Hong Kong and Macao in April and May 1962, when thanks to the temporary relaxation of exit controls, the normal steady trickle across the frontier became a flood in which over 60,000 refugees poured into Hong Kong within one month. When people leave their homes and possessions, the assumption must be that conditions have become intolerable and the outlook hopeless. Perhaps more significantly the bitter Sino-Soviet exchanges have revealed that some 50,000 to 70,000 Kazakhs and Urghurs crossed the Sinkiang border into the USSR.

No session of the National People's Congress, which according to the constitution should be an annual event, was called in 1961. In both 1962 and 1963 the Congress was confined to secret sessions. This is in striking contrast to earlier years, in which it was the occasion for publicizing claims to spectacular economic progress and plans for even greater achievements. The official communiques in both years have been uninformative and retrenchment policies are being continued.

During 1963, the beginning of a revival was claimed. Food conditions continued to improve, but the weather was again difficult and the increase in the grain harvest disappointingly small. Grain buying from the non-Communist world for 1964 has continued at as high a level as in recent years. Although there have been passing references to the third Five-Year Plan, which should have begun in 1963, it was not mentioned in the communique after the National People's Congress, perhaps the surest sign that despite some recovery in industry, or even progress in certain priority sectors such as oil and chemical fertilizers, no rapid industrial advance is planned for some time yet.

The theme of self-dependence was strongly emphasized during the latter part of 1963, as Sino-Soviet polemics became more acrimonious. The withdrawal of Soviet technical assistance is now blamed equally with the weather for China's difficulties since 1960 and less and less is heard of her own 'shortcomings and mistakes'. Now that the export position has improved somewhat, China is turning increasingly to the non-Communist world for the equipment, including complete plants, which she is in no position to provide for herself.

The rapidity of the population increase (said to be over 2 per cent annually) is now officially recognized as a threat to plans for raising living standards and a policy of family limitation is being actively pursued. The campaign is accompanied by various methods of coercion (such as forfeiture of certain family benefits) designed to encourage later marriage and a top limit of three children.

It is tempting to compare China's great economic difficulties with those of the USSR during the early 1930s, in that both countries were determined to industrialize as quickly as possible, even though this meant placing an intolerable burden on agriculture, and there was little or no hope of obtaining foreign help except what could be paid for by exports. But the main cause of the USSR's troubles during the first Five-Year Plan was the violence with which agricultural collectivization was put into effect. In China, after a cautious start, collectivization came quickly and, if the available reports are to be believed, relatively bloodlessly. It was apparently accompanied by a rise in grain and raw cotton output and in livestock numbers. However, apart from pigs and poultry, livestock are relatively unimportant in China, and the official figures are in any case suspect. In the USSR there had been a disastrous fall both in grain production and livestock numbers which led to mass starvation and the loss of millions of human lives. There was no going back on Soviet collectivization. China's troubles are directly associated with the Great Leap Forward and the communes, both of which came by means of mass psychological pressure, and with a prolonged series of natural disasters such as never confronted the Soviet Communists. It is arguable, however, that even without the Great Leap Forward and the communes, collectivization would, by now, have adversely affected the Chinese food and agricultural situations. In any case, the Chinese Communists have retreated, for the time being at least, both from the Great Leap Forward and the communes and have also reverted to something rather more primitive than the collectives. Does this denote greater flexibility than Stalin was capable of, or will it be only a matter of time before Chinese Communism is pushing the people into yet another mad rush to catch up with the industrialization of richer countries?

So great are China's problems that the retreat from the follies of the Great Leap Forward and of the communes would probably have been unavoidable even for the most hide-bound Stalinists, so too much should not be made of the flexibility of the Chinese Government. Indeed, if any guidance is to be obtained from the quarrel with the USSR, whose leader, Khrushchev, is distinguished from the Chinese by his relative flexibility, the latter may need only a couple of good harvests for them to resume their old policies. Their Communist fervour, to judge from their latest pronouncements, is undiminished, which means that, ideologically, they are committed to the planned economy with its emphasis on heavy investments and the rapid stimulation of the basic and heavy industries. The far greater industrial capacity of Western non-Communist countries is an ever-present temptation to them to relegate agriculture once again to its old place in the order of economic preference. If these considerations prevail, there may not be a reversion to the madness of 1958 which, in any case, went beyond what was demanded by Marxist orthodoxy, but there could be an economic policy which held out little prospect of material well-being for any Chinese alive today, pursued in the interest of military strength and of a doubtful prosperity for the great-grandchildren of the present generation. If China is to remain under her present régime, this seems to be the most likely prospect.

CHAPTER XI

The Economic Contacts of the Communist Countries with the rest of the World

In the examination of the significance and growth, and of the strengths and weaknesses of the Communist economies, relatively little attention has been paid to their impact on the rest of the world. If Khrushchev's boast that Communism will bury capitalism is to be vindicated without recourse to major military action, there must be contact between the Communist and non-Communist countries. Since the death of Stalin, increased emphasis has been laid by the former, particularly the USSR, on the development of such contacts. In the economic sphere, these have taken the two major forms of foreign trade and aid to under-developed countries, although it must be emphasized that the encouragement of trade between Communist and non-Communist countries has been by no means entirely for political reasons. While it is obviously politically advantageous to increase the dependence of under-developed countries on the USSR by trading with them, there are strong economic motives for trade expansion. For one thing the Soviet Union needs to obtain foreign currency to buy vital supplies of machinery and equipment from the industrial Powers of the West, not to speak of the benefits its economy receives from imports of food and raw materials from less developed areas. Its need for foreign currency has been increased by the grain purchases which it has had to make in the West since the autumn of 1963. In recent years it has never been able to finance its imports from the West entirely by commodity exports and the deficiency has been made good by selling gold. Its current abnormal requirements have meant that its gold sales have reached record levels. It is thus unwise to regard every new Soviet trade deal as a sinister political move.

Under Communism, foreign trade is a State monopoly generally

conducted within the framework of agreements between one Government and another. It is often hard to distinguish between trade conducted primarily for economic or primarily for political reasons, but
since nobody would enter into trade transactions without hoping to
gain something and, in Communist eyes, what is good for the economy is good for Communism, the distinction need not be laboured.

Under Stalin, the USSR went to great lengths to be self-sufficient
and encouraged a similar policy among its satellites, forcing them to
sever many of their trade relations with the outside world and to
confine their trade as far as possible within the bloc. This was for
political reasons and was costly economically. These measures were
imposed on the East European satellites mostly with the formation
of the Council for Mutual Economic Assistance (CMEA), which was
the USSR's answer to the Organization for European Economic Co-
operation. At about the same time the NATO countries banned the
export to the bloc of armaments and strategic materials and placed
restrictions on those of indirect defence value. Khrushchev's reversal
of Stalin's policy makes economic sense as well as helping Communism to make a greater impact on the rest of the world. This
outward-looking policy became manifest in 1954, when a beginning
was made both with more normal trade practices and with the more
purely political programme of economic assistance to under-
developed countries. With the help of Communist propaganda, a
stir has been caused by both these developments, but few in the West
seem to have realized how difficult it must be quickly to change the
traditional leaning towards self-sufficiency, especially when it is
partly the product of natural and historical circumstances.

FOREIGN TRADE

Foreign trade will be dealt with separately from development aid. In
monetary terms, it is far the more important. Khrushchev's policy
has been to expand Soviet foreign trade in general, primarily for the
sake of the benefits to his economy in the form of much-needed
imports of modern capital equipment and increased purchases of
essential raw materials such as natural rubber and copper, which are
unobtainable or scarce within the USSR, and perhaps only secondarily
for the impact such trade would make on the outside world. Certain
of the East European countries, such as East Germany and Czechoslovakia, have well developed capital goods industries whose products they would gladly sell outside the bloc for hard currency. The
growth of much of this type of satellite trade has been restricted,

however, because of Soviet insistence that producers should concentrate on meeting the needs of the USSR, as during the last years of Stalin. Thus, trade within the Communist bloc has continued to be developed at the expense of that between Communist and non-Communist countries, although both have grown fast.

Trade missions have been sent by the USSR and satellites to any non-Communist country willing to receive them. A conspicuous part has been taken in trade fairs throughout the world and there has been great activity in the establishment of agencies. The uncommitted countries, which largely correspond to the under-developed group and are mostly in Africa, Asia and Latin America, have received more of these approaches and have been, in general, more responsive than the main industrial countries. Some of them, such as Guinea or Egypt, have been only too willing to show their independence of the NATO Powers; others have been attracted by offers of capital goods hard to obtain elsewhere, or glad to dispose of primary produce which was doing badly on world markets. By the middle of 1961, there were well over 200 bilateral trade agreements between Communist countries and some thirty to forty non-Communist, mostly uncommitted countries.

According to the latest Statistical Year Book of the United Nations, the total foreign trade turnover (imports plus exports) of the Communist countries more than doubled between 1953 and 1962, from $15,710 million to $34,980 million.[1, 2] Taken in the context of world trade as a whole, this is not as impressive as it at first looks, since the latter rose during the same period from $166,900 million to $290,200 million.[1] Thus by 1961, the share of the Communist countries in world trade was still less than 12.1 per cent compared with 9.4 per cent in 1953—very little indeed for a group of countries comprising, with Communist China, some 35 per cent of the world's population. Moreover, since 67 per cent of the Communist countries' trade in 1961 was confined to transactions among themselves, their trade with non-Communist countries accounted for no more than 4 per cent of total world trade exclusive of that between one Communist country and another. The Communist countries still have far to go before their trade can have the economic impact promised by their propaganda.

[1] All dollar values and prices shown in this chapter for Communist trade and aid have been calculated by conversion of roubles at official exchange rates.

[2] Figures exclude trade of the Far Eastern Communist countries, China, North Korea, North Vietnam and Mongolia, amongst themselves, and also trade between East and West Germany.

The reasons why the Communist countries play the small part in world trade they do are obvious. Geography and climate have made them high cost countries industrially, and the gross inefficiencies of their system have aggravated this. North America and Western Europe are generally not interested in the finished products of Soviet industry mostly because of their old-fashioned design and poor quality. Even less sophisticated countries are often badly caught by the inferior quality of Soviet deliveries. For example, the despatch of several new fishing trawlers to Iceland was followed by mounting criticism of faulty construction, bad aluminium linings in the holds, defective auxiliary engines and poor quality ballast. Ghana has been badly disillusioned over Soviet passenger aircraft which, among other things, are excessively costly to run. Individual industries or enterprises outside the bloc look upon the Communist countries largely as potential markets, while Western European countries which import from them are chiefly interested in obtaining foodstuffs and primary produce such as timber, manganese, oil and pig iron. The Soviet need to obtain the superior capital goods of Western Europe is one of the main bases of the trade drive and Soviet primary products are almost the only acceptable means of payment. As shown earlier, the prices of these products inside the USSR can be phenomenally high compared with those in world markets, but unless the USSR enjoys certain powers of coercion over her trading partners, world prices have to be approximated if the bilateral transactions are to be concluded. For the most part, the world price or perhaps a little less, is used for exports from Communist to non-Communist countries; a notable exception is oil, which seems to be the spearhead of the Soviet trade drive. Both for crude oil, which accounts for more than half the weight of Soviet oil exports, and for refined products, the prices charged to customers in most independent countries are considerably lower than those of the big oil companies.[1] The European satellites, however, who are growing consumers of Soviet oil, have to pay far higher prices, sometimes nearly double those charged outside the bloc.[2] Finland, Iceland and Afghanistan are also denied cut prices for bloc oil, the Finns and the Afghans being small neighbours of the USSR whose whole economies are subject to Soviet

[1] The border price in West Germany for Soviet crude oil averaged $1.72 per barrel in 1961, against $2.12 for the cheapest non-Soviet crude and an average non-Soviet price of $2.56. Platt's oil gram, 7.XI.6.

[2] The average price in 1960 for Soviet crude oil was $1.56 per barrel in non-Communist countries.

pressure, while Iceland is beholden to the USSR for having relieved her of surplus fish supplies during her dispute with Britain.

With world energy consumption rising fast, the Communist countries have succeeded in increasing their exports of oil to the outside world from 6.6 million tons in 1955, of which the Soviet share was 4 million, to 30.5 million in 1961, almost the whole increase having come from the USSR. During the past two years these exports have risen more slowly—partly, it seems, for internal reasons and partly through failure to find large new markets in the free world. In either case it seems doubtful whether the former rapid progress can soon or easily be resumed. Before 1955, between 80 and 90 per cent of the deliveries outside the bloc were refined products, but by 1962 the share of crude oil had risen to 52 per cent and most of the refined products consisted of industrial fuels which could easily be marketed in bulk, without the need to establish elaborate distribution systems like those of the oil companies. Two-thirds of the oil is taken by Western Europe, particularly Italy, which has been attracted by the prices and by the opportunities for the sale of her exports in the USSR. It is ironical that Italy's rapid economic growth of recent years should have been facilitated by cut-price Soviet crude oil. However, Italy takes under a quarter of her requirements from the bloc, the only non-bloc countries which rely primarily on the Communist oil supplies being Finland (78 per cent in 1961), Iceland (88 per cent), Afghanistan (55 per cent), Guinea (70 per cent) and Cuba (100 per cent). The last two have come to rely on bloc oil purely for political reasons.[1]

The pattern of the Soviet oil export drive is thus clear—to cut the price where this is the best means of obtaining sales, as in most of Western Europe, and to exact as high a price as possible nearly everywhere where terms can be dictated.

Until recently, it seemed that the USSR was amply equipped to press forward with this policy. Its annual output of crude oil far exceeded its own and indeed the whole bloc's requirements. The fact that this output had outstripped refinery capacity was no disadvantage since the principal demand in the main markets, mostly well provided with their own refineries, was for crude oil rather than refined products. Among the refined products the best export outlet was for heavy fuel oil, and here again the Soviet refineries could provide a reasonable surplus. Their inability to turn out large quantities of, for example, motor spirit of the quality acceptable to western markets mattered

[1] In spite of her complete dependence on *bloc* oil, Cuba pays for Soviet crude oil at only about half the top rate charged to the European satellites.

little, since marketing and distribution facilities were nearly all under the control of the major oil companies, which would rule out the prospect of large bloc sales. Only in respect of diesel oil was the USSR at a disadvantage. In 1962 the tonnage of this fuel sold to the free world came third after crude oil and fuel oil, and in value it easily exceeded the latter. Here the Soviet refinery effort has been inadequate and the substantial exports were to some extent achieved at the expense of domestic requirements so as to secure badly needed foreign exchange. It should, moreover, be borne in mind that although the Volga/Urals area, which accounts for three-quarters of Soviet crude oil production and most of the exports, is among the remotest from ports or frontiers of any in the world, oil is more easily transported than most commodities by pipelines and tankers. In general, therefore, there was every reason to expect a rapid and continuous rise in the surplus of oil and oil products readily available for export to the free world.

In the past two or three years, however, the position has changed. The Soviet performance in oil prospecting has for some time fallen well below the planned levels and proved—as distinct from probable —oil reserves have failed to rise at the expected rate. These may soon curtail the hitherto rapid increase in crude oil production. There is little doubt that the Seven-Year Programme for oil production will be achieved and even slightly exceeded, but the handsome margin of over-fulfilment that formerly seemed likely now seems improbable. Much of the oil now produced abounds in sulphur and other impurities, to the distaste of refiners both at home and abroad. This applies particularly to Volga/Urals crude oil, much of which also tends to yield a deficiency of the diesel and fuel oil most urgently needed both at home and for export and a surplus of light products in relatively low demand. Again, oil consumption in the USSR has risen rapidly, notably of the products most required for export, and instances of Soviet unwillingness to exercise or even to fulfil export commitments have been reported. Finally, the Soviet oil salesmen have failed, since the deal with Cuba, to capture any large new foreign markets. For these reasons the expansion of Soviet oil exports—and hence of those of the bloc as a whole—has slowed down since 1961, and seems unlikely to regain its former tempo in the near future.

Nevertheless, the bloc is now exporting over 36 million tons of oil a year and the figure may well continue to increase by a few million tons annually. Despite the difficulties it seems clear that the USSR intend to increase it as fast as possible. As is indicated by the price differentials for sales within the bloc and to most non-bloc countries and the differences in Western Europe between Soviet and non-Soviet oil prices, much of this export business is likely to be transacted at a considerable financial loss. Indeed, it has been pointed out by a Middle East oil authority that the price for a barrel of Soviet crude oil at $1.10 f.o.b. Black Sea, compared with $1.66 for Arabian Gulf and Iranian crude, would be unlikely to cover transport costs.[1] However, hard currency or its equivalent value in raw materials and equipment are obtained in return, Western oil interests are embarrassed, and the impression created of Soviet ability to achieve conquests in trade as in the scientific and military spheres.

The possibilities of the USSR launching out into the world market with other products besides oil are limited. In the later 1950s it looked as if attacks would be made with such metals as aluminium and tin. These and most other commodities are much harder for the USSR to produce than oil. On the grounds of cost, available supply and transport, they could not be expected to have the impact outside the bloc that has been achieved, even though on a limited scale, with oil. One Soviet industry whose growth in relation to that in the non-Communist world has been even more spectacular than oil is iron and steel. It might, therefore, have been considered suitable as a trade weapon, but it has not yet been used. Soviet exports of iron and steel in 1962 amounted to little more than 6 million tons, of which 4 million tons were to other Communist countries. Of the 2 million tons exported to the outside world 50 per cent was pig iron, which is only once removed from the raw material stage, whereas such a producer as West Germany exports over 8 million tons a year, almost entirely rolled steel, and France and the Benelux group each export over 5 million tons. As with oil refining so with the rolling of steel, the USSR is unable to compete with the capacity and quality of Western Europe and North America. In the case of cold rolled sheets and tubes, it even sends much of its semi-finished steel to Western Europe for re-rolling and return to the USSR—which must be a costly undertaking.

The farther into the production process we go from the raw material stage the less likely are the Communist countries to be able to compete effectively on world markets without recourse to the coercive tactics used with such countries as Finland and Iceland or to price cutting which leads to an enormous differential between what is charged inside and outside the Communist bloc. This is not

[1] 'Open Letter' to the League of Arab States, March 1962, from M. Emile Bustani of the Lebanon.

only because of high costs but poor quality; it does not apply in the same measure to countries like East Germany and Czechoslovakia because they enjoy a more favourable geographical position and have undertakings and skills in the engineering and other finishing industries which were well developed before Communism took over. However, the products of the Soviet armaments industry cannot be lightly dismissed for, although those sold abroad are rarely of the latest design, they are acceptable to a good many countries. But they do not appear in trade returns.

Because the foreign trade of Communist countries is a government affair and because of the use of discriminatory prices and export subsidies, it is not necessarily a powerful weapon in the non-Communist industrial world. A few individual products can be subsidized to bring their prices down to the world level, but it would be impossible to organize competition in that way for the whole of the bloc's exports and so inflict severe and widespread damage. With the huge sums which are being spent on armaments, space research and various white elephants in agriculture and industry and a housing programme which is falling well behind schedule, the authorities already have enough on their hands, tempting though it would be to embarrass the North American and West European economies in a general trade war. Indeed, in the last year or so, the USSR has been tending to deplete her gold reserves so as to maintain the desired level of imports from the West of capital goods. In 1963, when there was a disastrous harvest and big imports of wheat, gold sales rose to between $400 million and $500 million, or considerably more than double the year's production. This does not suggest that the USSR is in a position to indulge in an anti-Western trade war.

As far as trade with the non-industrial countries outside the bloc is concerned, the going in a number of cases has been easier than elsewhere and for reasons already given. Thus, in 1962, more than 80 per cent of Cuba's trade was with Communist countries. This, however, is a special case. More typical examples are Afghanistan, Egypt, Syria, Guinea and Mali. At least 20 per cent of their trade turnover in 1962 was with Communist countries. Iraq, Indonesia, Burma, Cambodia, Iceland and Greece also rely heavily on their transactions with the bloc. Whereas the total trade turnover of the Communist countries more than doubled between 1953 and 1961, their turnover in transactions with the under-developed countries quadrupled during the same period to $3,400 million; it rose again in 1962 to $3,600 million. Even so, this accounted for only 6 per cent of the total trade turnover of the under-developed countries in 1962, as given by the United Nations. This was $60,200 million in 1962 (United Nations' *Monthly Bulletin of Statistics*, December 1963). A start has certainly been made in the development of trade between the Communists and the under-developed countries, but the way ahead is not an easy one. Particularly where Soviet equipment, other than armaments, is concerned, there is the need, frequently encountered, to compete with the mainly superior and more up-to-date Western European or American article and there is the growing and only partially satisfied demand within the bloc itself. More likely than not, the decisive factors which have won trade for the bloc have been political, or bloc willingness to grant credits to impecunious customer governments whose business does not particularly attract private firms in Western Europe or North America.

FOREIGN DEVELOPMENT AID

Unrequited economic aid in peace-time from one country to another is not a modern phenomenon. It originated in various of the more prosperous countries as famine relief, when it was organized mostly privately and by religious and charitable institutions. Large-scale aid for the rehabilitation or development of agriculture and industry dates from the Second World War, the closing stages of which saw the evolution of the United Nations Relief and Rehabilitation Agency. Most of the aid granted by UNRRA was American and in the form of foodstuffs, clothing and medical supplies, but it also included supplies of raw materials, fuel and equipment. It was followed by American and a little British interim aid and ultimately by the Marshall and allied American plans.

The Marshall Plan went seriously into operation in 1948 and was intended to be available to Communist countries as well as to those of Western Europe and their dependencies. Poland and Czechoslovakia showed initial willingness to participate, but the USSR refused to do so and compelled the Polish and Czechoslovak Governments also to refuse. Although the Marshall Plan insisted on one European country wherever possible helping another and was careful to give the recipient countries a full say in the use of the aid it distributed, it was primarily a means whereby the USA could furnish an unprecedented volume of unrequited economic aid to most of Western Europe. Not only did it provide far more than UNRRA, but its great emphasis on raw materials and capital equipment was, at the time of its inception, unique. Under various other programmes, the USA also helped not only the dependencies of Western European countries but

China, Japan, India, Pakistan and other non-European countries.

In due course, their economies on the way to rehabilitation, the Western Europeans also entered seriously into undertakings to provide economic assistance to needy countries in various parts of the world. Much of this aid was to former colonies of the Powers which provided it. An early example was the Australian-inspired Colombo Plan, under which she, Britain and other Commonwealth countries joined in providing mostly technical aid in South-East Asia. The USA subsequently joined and is playing a major part, and her Government aid to developing countries throughout the world continues to exceed that of all other contributing countries put together. By 1961, however, the dollar value of the flow of official aid from Western Europe and Japan was some 70 per cent of the annual value of Marshall aid between mid-1948 and mid-1952. Much of the aid granted to developing countries by the great non-Communist countries is frankly viewed as a means of fighting the growth of Communism. It is certainly seen in that light by the Communist countries themselves so, with the death of Stalin, it must have been inevitable that, when the USSR reviewed its approach to the outside world, it would wish to embark on a foreign aid programme of its own. The first foreign aid agreements between Communist and non-Communist countries were made in 1954, when the USSR and Czechoslovakia undertook to grant credits to Afghanistan worth the equivalent of $5.6 and $5 million respectively to finance capital goods and technical help. In the same year the USA furnished a total of $1,750 million worth of aid to other countries; $900 million went to Africa, Asia and Latin America—the regions generally regarded as uncommitted and under-developed.[1] With Western European countries beginning to emulate the USA, the Communist countries obviously had a long way to go to match the efforts of the non-Communists.

The Communist Powers naturally concentrated their efforts where the aid was likely to prove most effective or most useful from their own standpoint. Thus, Afghanistan bordered on the USSR and had, by the beginning of 1954, received $21 million from the USA since the Second World War,[1] which must have caused some concern to the Soviet authorities. In 1955 the USSR concluded only one aid agreement, but it was important—for $132 million with India providing for the start of a significant development in heavy industry. There were also Czechoslovak agreements with India, Egypt, Syria, Turkey and Argentina and an East German agreement with Indonesia. A big advance came in 1956 with the Soviet granting of a further $128

[1] *Statistical Abstract of the United States*, 1961.

million to India and $100 million each to Afghanistan and Indonesia, as well as several East European agreements and the beginning of Chinese aid, the latter to Cambodia, Nepal and Egypt. The sums promised during the year by the Communist Powers as a whole were equivalent to nearly $430 million—fifteen agreements in all—but in 1957 there was a sharp recession to little more than a third of this value. This may have reflected the pre-occupation of the whole bloc with the rehabilitation of Hungary after the severe damage inflicted during the uprising in 1956.

The ground lost in 1957 was more than made up in 1958, with the agreement between the USSR and Egypt worth $275 million, largely associated with securing the contract for the Aswan high dam and ancillary developments. This huge project had previously been discussed with Western consultants, and financial negotiations with the World Bank had reached the stage of agreement in principle when, after the Suez episode, a realization of the extent of Egypt's indebtedness to the bloc for arms caused the Bank to withdraw its offer. The USSR then stepped in, and at this point it seemed that the time might not be far off when the USSR would play the leading part in Middle East affairs. It was in July of the same year that the Iraqi royal family was assassinated, together with members of the Government, and the revolutionaries seized power under Brigadier Qasim. In March 1959, within a few months of the assassinations, the new Iraqi Government entered into an agreement with the USSR for the provision of armaments and of economic and technical aid. The development credit alone was worth $137.5 million and a further $45 million were promised in 1960, although sensible use of oil revenues by the deposed regime had already done much good to the country. However, the biggest Soviet undertaking of 1959 was to India for a further $420 million, mostly connected with the heavy industrial undertakings begun under the 1955 agreement. Also significant in 1959 were the USSR's agreements with Ethiopa—worth $100 million—and with Guinea, which was promised a credit worth $35 million. This was a sizeable sum for a small country, and was granted after she had refused to join the French Community or to have any treaty relationships with France and the latter had responded by withholding all economic support.

The sum of development credits promised by the whole bloc in 1959 approached $870 million, but in 1960 it reached as much as $1,170 million. Further important credits were then promised to India, Egypt, Iraq and Guinea, although the most interesting features were Ghana's acceptance of Soviet and Czechoslovak promises of

I

credits worth $40 and $3.7 million respectively; the large bloc promises to Indonesia totalling some $290 million; and promises to
Cuba totalling nearly $240 million. Both the latter also received
much war material. The Government of Ghana, a member of the
Commonwealth, had become increasingly neutralist; Indonesia was
preparing for her showdown with the Netherlands over western New
Guinea; Cuba and the USA had severed their close connections and
were entering into a state of virtual political and economic warfare.
Thus, in 1960 one of the characteristics of the Communist bloc's
approach to development aid was probably as clear as it had ever
been—to exploit the moves of Governments of Asia, Africa and
Latin America when their relations with North American or Western
European countries had seriously deteriorated.

The difficulties which arise between newly-independent countries
and the West may be fundamentally an expression of their independence but they tend to take the form of disputes over the amount
and the conditions of economic aid. Legitimate doubts of the pros-
pective aid providers about the feasibility of suggested projects make
them want to insist on safeguards. These can easily be interpreted as
attempted interference, and as insults to the integrity and capacity
of the developing country. Much is therefore made by the Communist countries of the claim that their aid is 'without strings'. What
appears to happen is that, having decided with the developing country
on the projects, the Communist country grants the necessary credit
and then sets about providing and erecting the equipment needed.
Technicians are sent to carry out the work or to supervise and to
train the local people, some of whom may also go for training in the
bloc country concerned. The credit is at a low rate of interest, this
being a feature of credits granted within the bloc. Repayment, mostly
in products of the developing country, does not begin until the works
is in production and will last about ten to twelve years, after which
the works will be the property of the receiving country. The freedom
from strings lies in this absolute ownership—as distinct from the
enterprise being the property wholly or partly of a foreign investor—
and in the absence of political stipulations.

Freedom to turn other than to the USA, Western Europe or the
mainly Western-financed international lending and economic aid
institutions for development credits has its attractions for developing
countries. The total 'demand' for development aid dwarfs the supply.
Thus, there has been ample room for the Communist countries to go
on expanding their development credits. However, the total amount
promised by them in 1961 was somewhat less than in 1960, a notice-

able drop in Soviet promises not being fully counterbalanced by a rise in those of the East European satellites and China. Several agreements still being negotiated at the end of 1961 were thought at one time to be likely to help in bringing about a resumption of the increase in 1962, but this did not happen. Instead, there was a further sharp fall in the amounts promised by the USSR, and a less substantial one in the case of Eastern Europe, while those undertaken by China and her satellites fell from $175 million in 1961 to $22 million in 1962. Her own severe economic difficulties will have contributed to the fall in the case of China, but this was hardly so for the rest of the bloc. However there was a fairly marked rise in Soviet and Chinese commitments in 1963, and in the first half of 1964 the total value of new commitments was already greater than those for the whole of the two preceding years together.

It takes several years to complete the kind of foreign development project undertaken, the time varying considerably according to the type of installation and to local conditions. Hydro-electricity schemes, iron and steel plants, and integrated oil establishments might, for example, require five years or more even under good conditions, light industry much less. At a guess, western contractors might require, for fixed investments as a whole, an average of three years. If this is used as a rough yardstick, by the end of 1961 total drawings since 1954 roughly equalled the value of promises made up to the end of 1958 in the case of the USSR and were well ahead of them in the case of the far smaller East European promises. So far, so good, but the value of Soviet promises made in 1959 and 1960 alone were each some 65 per cent greater than the total sums promised in the previous five years, while for Eastern Europe it was 65 per cent greater. Until then, yearly drawings on the USSR had probably fallen short of $200 million, while drawings on Eastern Europe had not risen much above the $50 million mark. For the general standard of fulfilment to be maintained, effective drawings on credits promised would soon have to be six or more times as great as in any previous year. In fact, drawings, especially on Soviet loans, have now increased considerably but to nothing like this magnitude. To a certain extent, this is explained by the nature of the works now being undertaken, many of which are civil or heavy engineering projects not scheduled to be completed in under five years. (The main seals in the Aswan dam are planned to take nine years.) But it was in the middle of 1961 that the USSR announced its intention drastically to increase defence expenditure and to hold up further cuts in the strengths of its armed forces. This must have profoundly affected the whole economy and the foreign development aid programme would not have been immune.

At the 22nd Communist Party Congress in Moscow in October 1961 Khrushchev devoted much time to the battle against colonialism and what he called 'neo-colonialism'. This could be defined as the continuance of western capitalist control of former colonial territories by indirect means, particularly trade and finance. Subsidies by the former metropolitan Power, western development aid and investment capital are all denounced as 'neo-colonialism' and contrasted to Communist 'aid without strings'. Khrushchev said at the congress that the Communists would continue to provide material help to the newly-independent countries. But he also said that taxation was shortly to be abolished and made fantastic promises about the age of plenty that was to begin for the Soviet worker by 1980, when he would enjoy a standard of living 75 per cent greater than that of workers in the USA today, including free feeding and housing. These and other such promises were made at the same time as the USSR was conducting some of her greatest nuclear test explosions and was rapidly expanding her expenditure on the space programme. It was only a few months later that the taxation promise was rescinded and it became clear that the housing programme was being curtailed. It is hardly surprising, therefore, that Soviet promises of development aid in 1962, although more numerous than ever, were but an eighth in total value of those made in 1960 and that, as far as can be judged, there was no spectacular improvement in the rate of drawings in that year, either by the USSR or Eastern Europe. On the other hand, Cuba must have represented a considerable diversion of effort in terms of aid. Bloc deliveries to that country financed by deficit credits on current trade must now exceed $600 million. It is also apparent from the latest figures that the Soviet Union may have stopped the downward trend in the granting of development aid. Whether this is permanent remains to be seen, but evidence that large sums will still be advanced under favourable circumstances is provided by Soviet offers of $800 million to India for her next Five-Year Plan. Credits and drawings to the end of 1963 are estimated to have been approximately as shown in the table opposite.

The apparently slow rate at which development credits granted by the USSR and Eastern Europe have hitherto been implemented is even more remarkable when it is considered that their deliveries of capital equipment to China have been greatly reduced since 1960 and their technical experts withdrawn. Pre-occupation with defence and internal economic development probably help as much to explain past sluggishness in the growth of the credit drawings as they do the drop in the amounts of the new credits granted. But that is not all. The ability of many of the developing countries to carry out their share of the planned installations is limited. There have been cases where a generous Communist credit has been promised but years have gone by without the creditor being called upon to do anything substantial in fulfilment. This may be due to planning difficulties at the receiving end or to dissatisfaction with the materials and equipment made available. Of the more important investments undertaken, progress has been good in Afghanistan and Iraq, as well as with the great Bilhai integrated iron and steelworks in India—a prestige project which could not be allowed to fail, as similar plants are also being erected in India by Britain and West Germany. Work on the Aswan dam is up to the revised and extended schedule, but it will not be until after its completion that it will be possible to judge

Creditor	Development Credits Extended		Estimates of Amounts Drawn	
	1963	1954/63	1963	1954/63
	(Millions of Dollars)			
USSR	220	3,560	300	1,170
East European Satellites	180	1,290	110	400
China and Satellites	90	525	10	90

whether western reluctance to undertake it was economically justified. However, neither India nor Egypt has been entirely satisfied with the working of the aid agreements as a whole, the former because of delays in delivering electricity generating equipment and the latter because of similar trouble over steelworks equipment. Argentine, Ethiopia and Indonesia are other important countries in which, for one reason or another, progress in the use of the economic development credits has been slow.

The significance of the Communist development credits cannot be fully assessed without comparing them with those granted by non-Communist countries. In the table which follows, it has been possible only to show yearly figures of the development credits promised by the Communists, the much lower figures of drawings being hard to assess annually. For the non-Communist countries, governmental and private long-term development funds are shown separately. Over 80 per cent of the former consists of 'grants and grant-like contributions'—in effect, free gifts. Only a tiny proportion of the Communist development funds have so far taken the form of grants, although the interest charged is low. But for this low interest they would be more comparable to the private funds provided by the non-Communist countries than to official aid.

It will be seen that the flow from the non-Communist countries both of private and of official capital has been substantial for many years, and though the annual figures shown in the table are not claimed to represent the amounts actually invested in the developing countries, they are unlikely to differ materially from them.

The contrast between the inevitably small total of development credits promised by the Communist countries and the flow to the developing countries of long-term financial resources from the non-Communists has always been significant. In 1956, for example, when the Communist programme was apparently forging ahead, the promises made under it were worth only one-eighth of non-Communist official aid and about one-sixth of the funds provided from private sources. By 1960, the peak year for Communist promises, these were still under one-quarter of official non-Communist aid and under one-half of private investments in the developing countries. By 1961, with the flow—official and unofficial —from the non-Communists still increasing, the ratios were about one-sixth and rather more than one-third, respectively. In 1962, Communist promises fell to one-sixteenth of official non-Communist undertakings and one-sixth of private loans. No comparison can yet be made for 1963, but it will still be overwhelmingly in favour of the West. In absolute terms, the gap between Communist promises of development aid and the non-Communist flow of development funds has been widening. Thus, in 1960, non-Communist official development aid exceeded Communist promises by over $3,700 million, but in 1962 the gap had increased to almost $5,600 million. The widening of the gap is, in fact, confined to official aid, reflecting both the growing concern of the leading non-Communist governments with the problems of the developing countries and the policy of ex-colonial Powers of providing support for their former colonies.

One last comparison is legitimate. If it is considered that, in 1963, the level of actual investments by non-Communist Powers in the developing countries was roughly equivalent to the total flow of funds in 1960, these investments are likely to have been some eighteen times the total drawings made by such countries on Communist credits. These figures speak for themselves. As with foreign trade, so with development aid, the Communist Powers must do a great deal more than hitherto if they seriously regard this as one of their more important means of burying capitalism.

ECONOMIC DEVELOPMENT CREDITS TO DEVELOPING COUNTRIES

(In millions of US dollars)

Communist Bloc Promises	Average 1950/55	1954	1955	1956	1957	1958	1959	1960	1961	1962	1963
USSR	23	6	132	355	117	408	862	810	550	100	220
Eastern Europe	3	5	16	33	24	126	93	246	305	258	180
China and Satellites	..	..	..	40	16	74	1	108	175	22	90
Total	**26**	**11**	**148**	**428**	**157**	**608**	**956**	**1,164**	**1,030**	**380**	**490**
Development Assistance Committee Countries (Flow of long-term financial resources)											
Official											
USA	..	..	..	1,996	2,083	2,388	2,310	2,817	3,493	3,606	
UK	..	..	..	205	234	276	375	402	441	417	
France	..	..	..	648	819	884	832	837	943	996	
W. Germany	..	..	..	149	300	278	337	324	589	427	
Japan	..	..	..	61	58	254	112	125	214	165	
Others*	..	..	..	147	259	205	266	331	335	346	
Total	**1,900**	..	..	**3,206**	**3,753**	**4,285**	**4,232**	**4,836**	**6,015**	**5,957**	
Private											
USA	..	..	..	..	..	..	..	1,040	1,038	914	
UK	..	..	..	..	..	..	..	432	423	420	
France	..	..	..	..	..	..	..	367	347	385	
W. Germany	..	..	..	..	..	..	..	221	212	255	
Japan	..	..	..	..	..	..	..	100	157	117	
Others*	..	..	..	..	..	..	..	422	459	352	
Total	**1,600**	..	..	**2,440**	**3,369**	**2,669**	**2,222**	**2,582**	**2,636**	**2,443**	
DACC **Grand Total**	**3,500**	..	..	**5,646**	**7,122**	**6,954**	**6,454**	**7,418**	**8,651**	**8,400**	

* The other Development Assistance Committee countries include Belgium, Canada, Italy, Netherlands and Portugal.
Sources: Communist credits compiled from world Press and broadcasts. DACC Assistance: *Development Assistance Efforts and Policies in 1961* (Organization for Economic Co-operation and Development—Paris); *Development Assistance Efforts and Policies, 1963 Review* (OECD), and other OECD publications.

CHAPTER XII

The Summing Up

This book began by quoting statements made by Khrushchev in 1959 that Communism was going to bury capitalism in what, if capitalism did not start a world war, would be a great political and economic contest between the two systems. There has been no lack of further boasts in the ensuing years. An attempt has been made to show how much economic strength lies behind these threats. The production races, so beloved of Khrushchev, have been shown to exaggerate the achievements of the USSR in relation to those of the USA, founded as they are on questionable data of the former's own choosing. It is, nevertheless, true that Soviet industrial growth rates today are generally faster than American ones and that if this relationship were to continue long enough the time might come when the Soviet industry would produce more per head of population than American industry.

According to Khrushchev, this is to happen as soon as 1970, or thereabouts, but it has been shown that official Soviet statistics, even when taken on their face value, afford no grounds for this promise. These statistics claim that the industrial output of the USSR rose by 88 per cent from 1945 to 1950, by 85 per cent between 1950 and 1955, and by 64 per cent between 1955 and 1960, while fulfilment of the Seven-Year Plan required a further increase of 48 per cent between 1960 and 1965. The increase that will ultimately be claimed for 1965 may be somewhat more than 48 per cent over 1960, but it will be well below the 64 per cent claimed between 1955 and 1960. In other words, without having to be scaled down to realism, the official statistics show that, as in non-Communist countries, Soviet industrial output is increasing by smaller and smaller percentage amounts. Yet Khrushchev would have it that production is to increase by as much as 78 per cent between 1965 and 1970. For this to be achieved, there would have to be a steady increase in the yearly percentage growth of industrial labour productivity as well as a much faster transfer than hitherto of workers from agriculture to industry. But again, the official figures fail to support Khrushchev, for they show that as in most other great industrial countries, the tendency is for the percentage increase in labour productivity to shrink. And it is not even planned to transfer from agriculture to industry anything like enough workers by 1970.

During the last decade, the Soviet authorities have set great store by automation as a means of restoring the high percentage increases in labour productivity of the immediate post-war years but, so far, the USSR has singularly failed in its attempts to exploit this possibility. Industrial production has risen fast mainly because of heavy investment, particularly in such growth industries as fuel and power, metallurgy and engineering, aided by a quickly growing population and an even quicker flow of young people from the country to industrial centres. The investments have provided mechanization, but little automation, which is quite another matter, and much of the development is a repetition of what began to happen in Britain towards the end of the eighteenth century and reached its height in the USA and Western Europe in the late nineteenth and early twentieth centuries. It is probably faster than elsewhere largely because the USSR can take advantage of techniques which were unknown in the earlier stages of world industrialization and mostly copied from other countries. It is also greatly helped by the power enjoyed by totalitarian regimes to determine wage rates, which are not allowed to rise faster than the growth of labour productivity and thereby frustrate the investment programme. Automation is far from being the brain child of the Soviet economic system as suggested by the official propaganda. Developments introduced well after the Second World War in the USSR had started elsewhere years earlier. The lead of the USA and Western Europe is increasing rather than diminishing. The priority given by the USSR to modern armaments production and to the space programme has greatly inhibited its prospects with industrial automation because of the demand created by the former for such important items as instruments and electronic equipment.

The study of individual Soviet industries only partly confirms the claims made about the growth of industrial output as a whole. Because of the rapid expansion of the oil industry, the output of fuel and power in 1965 may reach 95 per cent of the original plan. The shortfall is likely to be due to considerable under-fulfilment of the coal and of the ambitious natural gas plans. This is unlikely, however, to prevent the authorities from claiming, in due course, that the 1965 plan for total industrial output has been fulfilled. Economies in fuel and power consumption, particularly through the fulfilment of the electricity plan and the substitution of the more efficient oil and gas for coal, will help to bring this about, but the recent decision to scale down the total fuel and power plan for 1965 underlines the lack of realism in Khrushchev's plan for industrial output in 1970.

The growth of iron and steel output, although somewhat slower than it was, should still see the fulfilment of the original 1965 plan, but there are difficulties in producing satisfactory rolled steel, particularly sheets and tubes. The other metallurgical industries generally lag well behind plan, face severe problems and, in common with much of the iron and steel industry, suffer from excessively high cost linked with official refusal to take account of important geographical factors. The engineering industry, whose official figures of total production are believed to cover that of armaments, has expanded so fast that, on paper, it can claim a level of output in 1963 as high as was originally planned for 1965. But this is based on a value index of doubtful validity. The figures published on the output, in physical terms, of individual engineering items do not lend strong support to claims of progress quite so fast as this. An increase in the output of armaments such as is strongly suggested by the official figures of defence expenditure since mid-1961 would depress the rate of growth of many of the civil branches of engineering without seriously affecting total output. But, as Khrushchev himself has said, fulfilment of his promises for the future are partly conditional on no undue increase in defence production.

Strenuous efforts are undoubtedly being made both to modernise and to secure the rapid expansion of the chemical industry, but the plans to make up for its past neglect are over-ambitious and have had to be altered to meet the needs of agriculture. By western standards, it will long continue to look antiquated, and to fail to produce the desired level and quality of heavy chemicals and fertilizers, petro-chemicals, and plastics, pharmaceuticals, insecticides and pesticides. Indeed, the backwardness of so basic a Soviet industry and the technical and other problems with which it is faced make Khrushchev's boasts about overtaking the productivity per head of population of US industry look more than usually ridiculous.

Khrushchev's policy of giving much more attention than Stalin to the expansion of agricultural, foodstuff and consumer goods output and housing has brought about significant improvements in living conditions for most of the population. These are continuing, but the leeway to be made up is enormous and the increased attention recently given to armaments production, to the development of new weapons and to space, must be held partly responsible for the failure to make greater progress. Agriculture, which tended to stagnate after 1958 and had a disastrous year in 1963, still remains one of the worst problems. It retains some 45 per cent of the USSR's employed population. In the USA, under 11 per cent of those employed are in agriculture but their total output is considerably larger and of a much better quality than that of Soviet agriculture. It will be many years after 1970 before the USSR will be able to achieve comparable employment ratios to those of the USA. Only then will it be possible for it to think seriously of having an industrial output per head of population higher than that of the USA. Despite the improved investments in agriculture and other inducements offered to the farmer since the death of Stalin, it is becoming increasingly clear that the whole Communist approach to agriculture is wrong and that until it is abandoned there is little or no hope of the Soviet economy providing the age of plenty promised by Khrushchev at the 22nd Communist Party Congress.

The Soviet economy also suffers in comparison with those of the non-Communist industrial countries because of the extremely poor quality and high cost of much of its output. This is due in no small measure to the priority given to armaments and space, but Marxist refusal to recognize the value of market prices rather than central planning on a scale which is beyond the capacity of the planner, is probably a more important cause of the trouble.

Although Khrushchev's boasts about the speed at which the Soviet economy is overtaking that of the USA need not be taken too seriously, the fact remains that, within the last thirty-five years, and in spite of two disastrous invasions which seriously damaged its most important industrial and agricultural regions, the USSR has become the second largest industrial country of the world and is the only serious rival to the USA in the production of armaments. This rivalry includes nuclear weapons and missiles and the allied field of earth satellites and other space vehicles where, in many respects, the USSR appears to be ahead of the USA. It is also undeniable that the share of the earth's territory and population under Communist control is far larger today than it was in 1919, while that belonging to what is called the 'imperialist camp' has greatly diminished. However, 60 per cent of the world's land and some 57 per cent of the population belong neither to the Communists nor to the 'imperialists'. It is in these countries, mostly comprising Latin America, Africa, the

Middle East and Southern and South-East Asia, that, in the absence of a nuclear war, Khrushchev expects the struggle largely to be fought. Many people have been so impressed by the industrial progress achieved within a few years by the USSR, with forced saving, direction of investments, rigid control of labour and wages and various other means of coercing people into increasing their production, that they think that Communist methods are the right ones to raise the uncommitted countries out of their poverty. This belief is even held about agriculture.

It has been useful to observe the experience of countries which have only comparatively recently fallen under Communist control, to see just how they have fared when Communist methods have been applied to their economies. The first to which this happened were the East European satellites—East Germany, Poland, Czechoslovakia, Hungary, Rumania and Bulgaria as well as Yugoslavia and Albania which, though no longer satellites, are still ruled by Communists. At that time, none, except possibly Albania, was as undeveloped as the typical African or South-East Asian country and some, such as East Germany and Czechoslovakia, were much better developed than the USSR itself. They already possessed education, skills, industries, administrative systems and experience which provided a basis for further development. In industry this has been fast but lopsided and has so far provided little satisfaction to the working population. Certain non-Communist countries, such as Japan and Italy, whose natural resources are about as limited as those of Eastern Europe, have expanded their industrial output as fast as, if not faster, than Eastern Europe without depriving the worker of most material comforts or freedom of consumer choice. And in agriculture there have been the same dismal failures in the European satellites as in the USSR. Production is much lower than it should be and the farm worker loathes the whole system. The most telling fact is that Poland and Yugoslavia have largely turned their backs on collectivization and, though not without their agricultural problems, have generally achieved better results than the Communist countries which have not.

When China became Communist, she was much less developed than Eastern Europe, although she had far better natural resources. If the official veil of secrecy could be penetrated, she would probably afford a much better example than Eastern Europe of what Communism can do to a country when it tries to transform its economy from a mediaeval to a highly industrialized State within a few years. An attempt has been made to piece together the story of China's economic development since 1948. What emerges is not so badly authenticated as to be completely valueless. Clearly something is seriously wrong with a country which, within a year or so of claiming to be expanding industries faster than anywhere else in the world, clamps down on virtually all published statistics, greatly reduces imports and radically changes the composition of the remainder in favour of food at the expense of industrial equipment. Tens of thousands of refugees have fled abroad in search of a better life. The story appears to be an exaggerated version of the shortcomings characteristic of other Communist countries—excessive concentration on industry, particularly heavy industry, and monumental failure with agriculture, brought about in no small measure by official inability to win the co-operation of the farmer, as well as by great natural disasters.

It is not surprising that the bloc impact on the rest of the world in terms of foreign trade, with the exception of Soviet oil exports and Soviet readiness to import capital equipment from Western Europe, has not so far been very great. High costs due to severe geographical difficulties and to the inefficiency inherent in a centrally-planned economy which has turned its back on market prices are an important factor here. So is poor quality. Most Communist exports have to be heavily subsidised before they can hope to find a foreign buyer, and there are limits to what even a totalitarian country can do in providing such subsidies, especially when the people are being bled white by mounting armaments and space programmes. Even so, Communist bloc development aid for the uncommitted countries is surprising, and the picture is by no means so favourable to the NATO countries as the figures suggest.

The most important Communist aid, apart from that to India, has usually followed in the wake of trouble between the recipient and one of the NATO countries. Thus, Egypt, Irak, Indonesia, Guinea, Ghana and Cuba had already begun their disputes with some 'imperialist' Power before the Communist countries stepped in with their aid. The Communist thesis that 'imperialism' contains the seeds of its own destruction cannot be idly dismissed. Modern world history contains many examples of subject countries freeing themselves from the empire of one or other of the North Atlantic powers, only to be faced with the most serious of economic, social and political problems. All sorts of help is required, which, in the first instance, the countries concerned are most likely to seek from their former rulers. It takes little imagination to realise the possibilities of trouble between the two groups. The requests of the new countries in terms of money and equipment will probably be large, but their capacity to make good use of the aid and their willingness to accept advice are likely to be limited. Insistence by the former metropolitan Powers on the observance of even reasonable conditions can be misunderstood and helped by Communist propaganda, interpreted as 'neo-colonialism'.

Capital investment in, and the development of, almost any undeveloped country bring with them serious difficulties regardless of whether there is foreign interference or not. It is hard, too, for impatient political leaders with a western education and for western technical advisers whose practical experience has mostly been acquired in one of the highly developed North Atlantic countries properly to understand the problems of tropical communities still largely at the stage before the agrarian revolution.

When people accustomed to a simple way of life have to adapt themselves to modern agricultural and industrial conditions, it is difficult to avoid hardship and impinging on cherished rights. Then there is the problem of inflation, almost unavoidable if there is to be rapid development, but which can cause acute social unrest.

Furthermore, countries trying to integrate themselves into the world trading system face problems and disappointments due to causes beyond their control, such as fluctuations in world demand and in the terms of international trade. These difficulties are likely to be greater when a developing country has seriously begun to lift itself out of the mediaeval phase than when its economy is static. After all, Karl Marx wrote his strictures on capitalism when Western Europe was well on the way towards improved living standards. Cuba enjoyed material conditions, particularly in the towns, as good as anywhere in Latin America and certainly better than almost anywhere in Asia or Africa. These were largely due to help from the USA, but that did not prevent her from succumbing to Communism. Latin America as a whole is already far more developed than Africa or Asia, yet it would be an optimist who thought that the danger of a Communist revolution in one or more of its States was less than in the other two continents.

The Communist countries are under much less pressure to grant development aid than their rivals. They may well have decided that in view of the growth in their defence expenditure, their best strategy is to sit back and wait for the economic and political troubles of Africa, Asia and Latin America to multiply of their own accord, rather than to devote large resources to help governments which are not even Communist. Indeed, generous Soviet economic assistance might conceivably delay the development of more Cubas, or of Communist take-overs in newly-independent countries. Thus, more unrest could see a resurgence of development aid from the Communist countries but only after it was quite clear that Communists were effectively in control of the countries to receive it. The foundation in recent years of colleges and universities in the USSR and elsewhere in the bloc to indoctrinate foreign students could be a much more serious threat than Soviet development aid. Reports on the troubles of Africans in these establishments show that they may be a two-edged weapon but it is not known how many students are becoming good Marxists and will in due course go home to exploit the social and economic problems of their native countries. Nor can it be assumed that the early mistakes made in these institutions will be repeated.

Thus, any satisfaction gained from realising how exaggerated are Communism's claims to economic strength and efficiency should be tempered by an appreciation of the size and complexity of the problems of providing aid to the developing countries. If Khrushchev's confidence that they will sooner or later be absorbed into the Communist world is to be confounded much thought and energy will have to be devoted to the problem for a long time to come.

It should be encouraging to recall the success of the Marshall Plan little more than ten years ago. In 1947, the strength of Communism in certain West European countries was so great and economic conditions were so serious that what subsequently happened in Czechoslovakia seemed likely to occur west of the Iron Curtain. American awareness of the dangers led to the Marshall Plan. Besides the ample provision of funds, some of the best brains of the United States, both from business and from the administration, were devoted to helping Western Europe to achieve economic rehabilitation. Within less than five years, what looked like imminent collapse was transformed into the strength that now makes Western Europe a more significant factor in world economic affairs than the much vaunted Communist economies.

Similar efforts by the USA to help Nationalist China were too late in materialising and too small to prove effective. So, today, in spite of its many shortcomings, Communist China is the principal source of danger to non-Communist South-East Asia, whose every weakness, political, military or economic, is being exploited. China is also turning her attention to Africa. Fortunately, people throughout the non-Communist world have had the opportunity to see for themselves the dangers of ignoring the Communist threat, although far too few seem yet to be willing to take advantage of it. If Khrushchev and his allies do succeed in 'burying' us it will not be because we lack the material means to avoid such a fate but because of a failure to use them. It is a source of encouragement that many countries as well as the USA have become involved in helping the developing countries and that through such voluntary organizations as Oxford Famine Relief and the Freedom from Hunger Campaign, private individuals are taking an increasing interest, but much more remains to be done before the situation can be viewed with confidence. It is indeed sobering that, in 1964, when economic conditions in the USSR are passing through a difficult phase and when the British and American economies are enjoying considerable growth, this tilt in the balance in favour of the west is not reflected in current developments in South-East Asia, Africa and Latin America. Our economies are undoubtedly far better equipped than those of the Communist countries to provide the means of material salvation in the three great uncommitted continents but there is a long way to go before we can fully exploit this advantage.

The Soviet Index of Gross Industrial Output

There are two possible sources of exaggeration in Soviet statistics. One is the deliberate falsification of production figures by such people as factory directors, farm chairmen, and local Party officials, and the other is the use of faulty statistical methods. Although tampering with output figures is common practice in the Soviet Union the resulting distortion is probably not great. For one thing, large-scale cheating tends to be self-defeating in Soviet conditions. The doubts voiced about the validity of the index of gross industrial output, however, lead to the belief that here is an inflation of quite a different order.

The official gross output index is a price-weighted aggregate of the value of industrial output of all enterprises. Considerable double-counting occurs in that the value of intermediate products transferred from one factory to another is added to the value of the final products. The total volume of production is therefore made to look larger than would be the case if a conventional western value-added method were used. More important are the distortions that affect the *rate* of growth. The reasons for such inflation are technical. Until 1950 the price-weights used in the index were those for 1926/7. This gave undue emphasis to the fastest growing sectors of industry. Then there was the problem of new products which were normally introduced at current prices, or an artificial estimate of 1926/7 prices. This led to an upward bias in the index because these prices were far higher than 'true' 1926/7 prices. A further point is that changes in the organization of industry produce fluctuations in the output index which are not connected with variations in real output. As output is aggregated at factory level, a vertical disintegration of production could result in a large increase in the value of gross output

Several independent estimates have been made by western analysts to arrive at a more accurate assessment of Soviet industrial growth.

K

The official Soviet statistics claim that between 1926 and 1955, industrial output rose twenty-one times. The best performance that any western study will allow is an increase of twelve times,[1] although some say it is only half that. It is fairly obvious that the official index is exaggerated, but by how much will probably never be known. All that can be said is that progress has not been as incredibly fast as the official figures show. But it is also likely that the degree of inflation has decreased, and that the index, say for the last decade, is a closer approximation to reality. A Soviet source[2] indicates that whereas gross industrial output rose 9.6 per cent in 1960, it was nearer 8 per cent if reworked on a western value-added basis.

[1] Seton, *Soviet Industrial Expansion*, Manchester Statistical Society, 1957.
[2] *The National Economy of the USSR*, 1960.

APPENDIX II

The Modern Armaments and Space Vehicle Race

In the annual budgets of most Communist countries, it is usually stated how much is to be spent on defence in the coming year and sometimes how much was allegedly spent in the preceding year. No statistical details are given, whereas in western countries such as Britain and particularly the USA, the breakdown of much of the defence expenditure is given in great detail. However, the Communist figures are often huge and their fluctuations from year to year are consistent with the known trend of events, so it would be unwise to dismiss them as fabrications. In the case of the USSR, Khrushchev's statement early in 1960 on the strengths of the armed forces in certain years was illuminating. Like those in the budgets, the variations in these figures were consistent with the trend of world affairs. Study of Soviet textbooks on national finance and of various other published statements, such as the annual budget speech of the Soviet Finance Minister, provide certain indications of the scope of the country's official defence figures. Lastly, there is the evidence of the annual military and air force displays in Moscow and other capitals of the bloc, and claims of achievements with weapons and space vehicles, much of which can be scientifically substantiated or refuted by the West. This overt information indicates a substantial military effort.

By a systematic recording and anlaysis of the available scraps of information and by studying the more voluminous western information for the sake of the analogies, it is possible to throw a good deal of light on the defence activity of Communist countries. For simplicity, attention will be confined to the USSR. This is justifiable, since it is the leading military Power in the Communist bloc as well as the one about which there is the most information.

It is assumed that such statements as are made by the Soviet authorities and used in this analysis are basically true, and that the official practice is to withhold information altogether rather than to publish statements which are blatantly false and therefore liable to be exposed. This approach may seem risky but it is important to know what emerges from an examination of what the USSR says about itself.

Scope and Size of Published Soviet Defence Outlay
According to the available data[1] the official figures of defence expenditure would appear to cover the following:

> weapons, ammunition, motor vehicles, equipment, engineer stores, fuel and power, service construction, the pay and maintenance of uniformed personnel, military academies and general administration.

Service pensions are probably excluded as are stockpiling, civil defence and the security services. The great bulk, if not the whole, of defence research and development is almost certainly excluded, as are investments in the armaments industry. In Britain and the USA, the defence figures always include considerable sums for research and development as well as outlays on government owned ordnance works, naval shipyards, etc. In the USSR, most of the former expenditure is covered by the large outlays on 'science' most of which, ironically enough, appear in the budget under the general title 'Social and Cultural'. Again, no details are published. Disclosures are also made about additional expenditure on science outside the scope of the official budget. In the calendar year 1960, which happens to have more satisfactory data about Soviet defence activity than for subsequent years, the USSR claims to have spent 9,310 million roubles on defence. At the official rate of exchange of 1.12 roubles to the pound sterling quoted by the Soviet authorities for 1960, this was equivalent to £8,300 million. In the financial year beginning in April, 1960, the British defence vote, excluding research and development was £1,401.6 million, or little more than one-sixth of the roughly corresponding Soviet defence expenditure, since little was invested by the British government in its ordnance plants and naval shipyards.

It may be contended that this official exchange rate is meaningless because, for example, comparison of Soviet and British retail prices shows that, for consumer goods, the former are so high that a rate of about 3.5 roubles to the pound was nearer the truth in 1960. But

[1] See in particular Skachko's *Biudzhet mira i biudzhet voini*, Moscow, 1958.

when official Soviet prices of engineering products are compared with their British equivalents, something approaching the official exchange rate is indicated—about 1.2 roubles to the pound in 1960, though with wide variations from product to product. Armaments are in the sphere of engineering, so use of the official exchange rate is not so ridiculous as it at first appears. It must be conceded, however, that the Soviet forces are big consumers of foodstuffs, clothing and other consumer goods which are priced very high. If it is assumed that about one-third of the total published defence outlay is accounted for by high priced consumer goods and the remainder by the much lower priced items of the engineering group, a 'defence rouble' for 1960 of about 1.5 to the pound sterling is arrived at. The official Soviet figures for the 1960 defence budget would then have been equivalent to 6,200 million, or nearly four-and-a-half times the corresponding British defence outlay. This is still a large sum, for though the Soviet population is over four times the British, its national income is less than three times. Under peace-time conditions in democratic countries, the lower the standard of living, the smaller would be the proportion of national income the people might allow the government to spend on defence. Thus, the amounts the USSR claims to spend for this purpose are relatively considerably higher than would be tolerated by the British electorate. Why should it be assumed, therefore, that the Soviet budget grossly understates the true expenditure directly allocated to defence?

A more detailed comparison should be made with the USA rather than with Britain. The USA has long announced her defence expenditure every year, giving many particulars not only of direct defence activity[1] but on military research and development, astronautics and the atomic energy programme. She also announces her service strengths annually and in some detail. Most can be learned from a comparison of Soviet and American figures over the whole post-war period. It is unfortunate that the Soviet authorities are not as explicit about expenditure on military research and development as they are considered to be about direct defence expenditure. The table that follows, therefore, can provide only a partial comparison. In the case of the USSR, calendar years are used, whereas US expenditure is for the twelve months ending on June 30 in the year shown.

---

[1] Direct defence expenditure is used as a convenient way of distinguishing between such expenditure as it is believed to be defined in the published defence votes of the USSR, which exclude defence research and development, and total defence expenditure as defined in the USA.

These figures can be regarded as the broad statistical background to the post-war Soviet/American dispute. In 1945, the American forces were slightly larger than the Soviet, but they were rapidly demobilised so that by 1946 they were already little greater than the Soviet forces were to be in 1948.

By then, the Soviet forces were about double the American. The total Soviet defence outlay, other than on research and development and the atomic energy programme, was still more than half the 1945

Year		USSR Direct Defence Outlay (Thousand Million Roubles)	Service Strengths (Thousands)	Direct Defence Outlay	USA Total Defence Outlay* (Thousand Million Dollars)	Service Strengths (Thousands)
1945		12.82	11,365	...	81.2	12,123
1946		7.66	...	...	43.2	3,031
1947		6.64	...	...	14.4	1,583
1948		6.63	2,874	...	11.8	1,446
1949		7.92	...	...	12.9	1,615
1950		8.29	...	...	13.0	1,460
1951		9.39	...	20.7	22.4	...
1952		10.86	...	37.8	46.0	...
1953		10.78	...	42.2	51.8	3,555
1954		10.03†	...	38.9	47.9	3,302
1955		10.74	5,763	34.1	42.1	2,935
1956		9.73	...	34.3	41.8	2,806
1957		9.67	...	36.7	44.4	2,796
1958		9.36	...	37.3	44.1	2,601
1959		9.37	3,623‡	38.4	46.2	2,504
1960		9.30	...	37.4	45.7	2,476
1961	original	9.26†	...	38.6§	47.5	2,484
	revised	11.60				
1962		12.70	...	40.4§	51.1	2,806
1963		13.90†	...	41.7†§	53.0†	2,703†
1964		13.30†	...	43.9†§	55.4†	2,695†

* Includes direct plus defence research and development, Atomic Energy Programme, Mutual Security Programme and stockpiling; but excludes expenditures by NASA on the space programme.

† Budget forecast.

‡ At end of year.

§ Figures for these cover a somewhat narrower range than those up to 1960, owing to elimination of certain research and development items which had previously been classified as direct defence expenditure under the military procurement headings.

amount, whereas the American, including research and development
and the atomic energy programme, was only 14.5 per cent. These
figures reflect the contrast between Soviet post-war bellicosity and
American pre-occupation with a rapid return to a normal peace-
time way of life. That Soviet defence outlay should have fallen so
much slower than forces strengths is consistent with the view that the
USSR was maintaining a high level of armaments production. In view
of the severity of Soviet war losses, this is striking evidence of
Stalin's capacity to give priority to defence activity when civil needs
were desperate.

The year 1948 saw a dangerous worsening of international tension
and the beginning of the Berlin air lift. Khrushchev did not disclose
Soviet strengths between then and 1955, but it can be seen from the
figures of defence expenditure that the USSR took the lead in military
preparations before the Korean War, which was launched by her
North Korean satellite in the summer of 1950. The Soviet outlay rose
by 25 per cent between 1948 and 1950, whereas the American rose by
only 10 per cent from a smaller total. Thereafter, of course, when the
USA realised Stalin's intention, both her defence expenditure and her
forces strengths increased spectacularly, reaching their maximum
in 1953. By 1955, when Khrushchev first announced his intention of
cutting strengths, Soviet defence expenditure was almost as great as it
had been at the height of the Korean War, whereas the roughly
corresponding American defence expenditure had already fallen by
20 per cent and her forces strengths by 620,000, or over 17 per cent,
in two years.

After 1955, the comparison becomes most interesting. The
Korean War was by then a thing of the past, Stalin had been dead for
two years and Khrushchev, with his more flexible ideas, was in the
ascendant. Soviet strengths were reduced by as much as 37 per cent
in four years and defence expenditure by 13 per cent. In the USA, on
the other hand, though the reduction continued, it was more gradual,
so that by 1960, forces strengths were still higher than in 1948 by just
over a million. Even so, Soviet strengths exceeded those of the USA
by over 1,100,000 and were also well-above the 1948 level. Both
countries were spending far greater amounts on defence in 1960 than
in 1948—the USSR, 45 per cent more directly on defence, the USA
nearly four times as much directly and indirectly. Moreover, after
1956, US expenditure tended to rise again despite the continuing fall
in strengths, and Soviet defence expenditure showed little inclination
to fall any further. These figures indicate that, in the late 1950s, both
countries were spending an increasing proportion of their defence

votes on the latest types of weapon and, in the case of the USA, whose expenditures on defence research and development and the Atomic Energy Commission are known, these classes of indirect defence activity expanded much faster than the rest. The same must have been true of the USSR, whose nuclear explosions and successes with guided and ballistic missiles and space vehicles could not have been achieved without vast and rapidly mounting expenditure. This is confirmed by the official Soviet figures of expenditure on 'science', which will be discussed in more detail later.

So much, for the time being, for the trends; what of the absolute defence expenditure? The conversion of dollars into roubles with inadequate information is difficult. According to the Joint Economic Committee of the US Congress, whose report *Comparisons of the United States and Soviet Economies* is a serious attempt by responsible economists to arrive at the truth, the rouble/dollar ratio for direct defence expenditure was probably about 0.45 roubles per dollar in 1955.[1] But there has been a fairly marked rise in US prices since 1955—20 per cent in the case of engineering products by 1960—and certain Soviet prices have also risen, though, it is believed, not so much. This probably warrants the use of a ratio for defence expenditure in the latter years of 0.4 roubles per dollar. Assuming this to be so, then in 1960, the USA must have spent the equivalent of 15,000 million roubles on direct defence expenditure compared with 9,300 million roubles by the USSR. That the USA may have been spending over 60 per cent more than the USSR on direct defence expenditure alone cannot have failed to impress the Soviet leaders, but it is fair to point out that, in 1948, the USSR was probably spending on direct defence activity 25 per cent more than the USA was spending both on direct and indirect activity. And, by 1950, Soviet direct expenditure probably exceeded American direct and indirect expenditure by over 40 per cent. The conclusion to be drawn is clear. The USSR under Stalin, with its economy seriously weakened by war, nevertheless considerably outdid the defence activity of the USA, with her powerful economy. But when finally provoked into rearmament, the USA was able quickly to leave the USSR far behind. Khrushchev, after the failure of the Korean adventure and with internal economic problems of his own, made some attempt to limit defence activity after the excesses of the early 1950s, but he has failed to induce the USA to revert to her 'pacifism' of the late 1940s. Nor can the USA altogether be blamed for this when account is taken

[1] This is the geometric average of 0.5 roubles per dollar with US weights and 0.4 roubles per dollar with Soviet weights.

of the events in Hungary in 1956 and of the USSR's boastful achievement with inter-continental ballistic missiles and space vehicles since
the summer of 1957. and more recently with claims of an effective
antiballistic missile.

Comparison of Soviet and US Direct Defence Expenditure
Although the Soviet authorities publish only total direct expenditure
annually, it is possible with the help of the figures of strengths for
certain years to exploit this information in such a way as to obtain
a sound appreciation of what lies behind the published data. In doing
this, the American data are of great help. These show annually what
is spent on personnel, weapons and equipment by broad category,
operation and maintenance, military construction and various
smaller items.

Details of direct expenditure on defence by the USA are shown
below. The figures exclude stockpiling and the mutual aid programme, for such expenditure is believed to be excluded in the
Soviet defence figures. Particulars are given for 1953, when US
strengths were at their maximum, and for 1955 and 1960, since for
the latter two years, Soviet figures both of strengths and of direct
defence expenditure are available.

DIRECT DEFENCE EXPENDITURE OF THE USA

	1953	1955	1960
		($000,000,000's)	
Personnel	11.6	10.6	11.7
Major Procurement ..	17.3	13.3	14.8
Aircraft	7.4	8.0	6.5
Missiles	0.3	0.7	3.8
Ships	1.2	1.0	1.7
Atomic Weapons* ..	0.2	0.3	0.5
Other	8.2	3.3	2.3
Military Construction ..	1.9	1.6	1.6
Operation and Maintenance	10.4	7.9	10.2
Other	1.4	1.0	−0.4
Total	**42.6**	**34.4**	**37.9**

* Transferred for purposes of this book from the Atomic Energy Figures.

Points to note are that personnel has been absorbing an average of
nearly 30 per cent of direct defence expenditure, major procurement
(of weapons and equipment) somewhat under 40 per cent, and
miscellaneous items (mainly operation and maintenance) about one-
third. If Soviet defence expenditure could be examined in the same

L

detail, it would almost certainly be found that it could be classified in this way, with personnel and weapons and equipment each absorbing a large proportion, yet leaving another large proportion for operation and maintenance and other miscellaneous items. For the sake of the light the US figures can throw on the Soviet, the major categories are each examined below.

Personnel

Although US strengths were reduced by 30 per cent between 1953 and 1960 the ratio of direct defence expenditure absorbed by personnel costs has increased. This is because the yearly cost per man rose from $3,263 in 1953 to $4,727 by 1960. Several factors are responsible for this increase. First, when strengths are cut, the proportion of better paid, senior ranks increases appreciably. Secondly, with the rapid advance of technical warfare, the proportion of posts with special proficiency supplements has been increasing. Thirdly, the pay of all ranks has had to be raised because of the rise of civilian incomes. The first two factors are likely to have affected the average service pay in the USSR as much as in the USA, but the third very much less.

Major Procurement

There was a big drop in the American outlay on weapons between 1953 and 1955, concentrated almost entirely on land armaments. In this period, the outlay on missiles and nuclear weapons began to increase appreciably as did, surprisingly enough, that on aircraft. In the following five years, the outlay on missiles and nuclear weapons increased 4.3 times but by 1960 aircraft still accounted for nearly half the total. The decline in expenditure on land arms continued, but there was a marked rise in the case of ships, which probably reflected the growing importance of atomic and missile launching submarines. The total cost of major procurement as a whole increased by 11 per cent between 1955 and 1960, but since the US prices of machinery rose by 20 per cent during the same period, there must, in fact, have been a fall of about 7.5 per cent in total defence production.

Miscellaneous Expenditure

The ratio of direct defence expenditure absorbed by operation and maintenance decreased slightly in the two years after the Korean War. This is understandable. But it subsequently increased so that by 1960 it was above the 1953 level. This is a reflection of the growing complexity and cost of operation of the military machine. The USA is lavish in her expenditure in this branch of military activity and probably devotes to it a considerably higher proportion than the USSR. Nevertheless, since this development is closely associated with the mechanization and modernization of the forces, the USSR must also be faced with a similar problem.

Soviet Direct Defence Expenditure

A good start in comparing Soviet and American defence expenditure can be made by estimating the total cost of personnel with the help of the figures of forces strengths given by Khrushchev for 1955 and 1960. The average cost per man can be assumed to have been about the same as the average income of civilians. In 1960 this was equivalent to about 80 roubles a month for all classes, including the highest officials, but excluding collective farm members, whose payment is partly in kind but whose living standards are much lower than the rest. It is hard to believe that the average amount spent per serviceman in the USSR could have gone far below this without impairing the efficiency of a priority calling. Allowance must now be made for the probable rise in cost per man between 1955 and 1960 for reasons roughly similar to those that applied in the USA. Mainly because of slower increases in living standards than in the USA it seems reasonable to consider that the Soviet increase was about a quarter, with the average cost per serviceman amounting to the equivalent of about 768 roubles a year in 1955 and 960 in 1960. Hence, with 5,763,000 men in the forces in 1955 and an average of 3,323,000[1] in 1960, the allocation of direct defence expenditure in the two years could have been roughly as follows:

	1955	1960
	(Thousand Million Roubles)	
Personnel	4.43	3.19
Major Procurement		
Operations Maintenance and		
Miscellaneous	6.31	6.11
Total	**10.74**	**9.30**

The figures suggest that although Soviet strengths were cut by

[1] Khrushchev said there were 3,623,000 at the beginning of the year but that during that and the next year they were to be reduced by 1,200,000.

about 42 per cent between 1955 and 1960 the outlay on weapons and equipment, operations and maintenance fell only slightly. Had this not been so, the Soviet authorities would have cut their total direct defence expenditure much more than they did. It is fairly certain, too, that this consistently high expenditure on armaments was because of the production of such weapons as missiles and nuclear devices. During the first half of the 1950's, the armaments output of both the USSR and the USA consisted almost entirely of conventional weapons such as were being produced or had been developed by the end of the Second World War, but research and development work was going on in both countries with a new generation of weapons. It logically follows that during the period of large-scale demobilization after the death of Stalin, there would be considerable surpluses of the kinds of weapon which were used in the Korean War. And the emphasis of armaments production would quickly change in favour of the latest types, notably guided and nuclear weapons. This tendency is quite clear in the American figures. Thus, between 1953 and 1960, the American expenditure on weapons and equipment other than missiles and nuclear weapons fell by 38 per cent.

All the available information points to a similar development in the USSR. Its various official claims and statements and the annual military and air displays in Moscow all testify to a waning interest in conventional weapons and a growing emphasis on guided and ballistic missiles. Thus, it will be recalled that during his visit to Britain in 1956, Khrushchev was scornful of the value of cruisers and that the first claim to have fired an inter-continental ballistic missile was made by the USSR in August, 1957. And at the beginning of 1960, when he said that Soviet strengths were to be reduced by a further 1,200,000 during the next two years, Khrushchev was most emphatic that fire power would not be impaired but would, in fact, increase.

Soviet direct defence expenditure, other than on personnel, in 1955 and 1960 can be sub-divided as for the USA, making allowance for the greater Soviet rundown in strengths. In the table which follows, it is assumed that the proportion spent by the USSR on operation and maintenance and miscellaneous items is less than in the USA, but tends to rise.[1] It is also assumed that the fall in outlay on conventional weapons has been somewhat faster than the cuts in

[1] In the USA the ratio of operation and maintenance and miscellaneous expenditure to total direct military expenditure other than personnel has been: 1953—44 per cent, 1955—44 per cent, and 1960—47 per cent. It is most improbable that the USSR would be so lavish as the USA, so it is assumed that the Soviet ratio was 35 per cent in 1955 and 40 per cent in 1960.

strengths.[1] Expenditure in 1955 on the procurement of missiles and nuclear weapons, is taken as 7.5 per cent of total procurement. In that year, it was 5.4 per cent in the USA. The assumption of a higher percentage for the USSR is consistent with its having been the first to succeed in launching an inter-continental ballistic missile.

ESTIMATED DISTRIBUTION OF SOVIET DIRECT DEFENCE EXPENDITURE BY MAJOR CATEGORIES

	1955	1960
	(Thousand Million Roubles)	
Personnel	4.43	3.19
Major Procurement		
Aircraft, Ships, Land Arms and		
Equipment	3.79	1.89
Missiles and Nuclear	0.31	1.78
Operation, Maintenance and		
Miscellaneous	2.21	2.44
Total	**10.74**	**9.30**

If the table accurately describes Soviet defence activity, it implies that, although Soviet direct defence expenditure in 1960 was probably little more than 60 per cent of that of the USA, the USSR may have allocated at least as much as the USA to the procurement of missiles and nuclear weapons. This conclusion is based on the fact that, although the USSR claims to have cut its strengths between 1955 and 1960, it has admitted only a modest diminution in direct defence expenditure. Furthermore, it is consistent both with the USSR's having succeeded in firing an inter-continental missile considerably earlier than the USA and with the confidence evinced by Khrushchev in Soviet striking power with such weapons.

Nevertheless, according to the same calculations, about as much continued to be allocated by the USSR for the procurement of conventional weapons and equipment as for missiles and nuclear weapons; and the sum was still a large one. This takes into consideration such official claims as those made by Marshal Malinowski in his speech at the 22nd Party Congress, when he was at pains to emphasise the USSR's strength with unconventional weapons as well as with conventional forces. It must not be forgotten, of course, that this

[1] In the USA a 30 per cent cut in strengths was accompanied by a 38 per cent cut in outlay on aircraft, ships, land arms and other equipment. A 42 per cent cut in Soviet strengths is assumed to be accompanied by a 50 per cent cut in outlay on these items of procurement.

estimated division of expenditure between conventional and unconventional weapons is only an estimate. What is most probable is that the combined outlay on weapons and material of both kinds has not fallen since it reached its Korean War peak.

Soviet Direct Defence Outlay Since 1960

The picture becomes confused after 1960 because of Khrushchev's announcement of far-reaching changes in defence policy in July, 1961. Direct defence expenditure was originally to have been 9,260 million roubles for that year, but the vote was raised to 12,390 million roubles, and at the same time all further cuts in strengths were stopped. It has since been revealed that the actual amount disbursed for defence in 1961 was 11,600 million roubles. If expenditure had proceeded as originally planned during the first half of the year, the increase during the remaining six months would have been by as much as 50 per cent. This was over three times more than would have been needed to support the servicemen who should have been demobilised between July and December, and suggests an increase in expenditure on military hardware which it is hard to believe the engineering industry could have furnished in so short a time.

Remembering that all this happened at the time of the tense Berlin crisis, it is tempting to conclude that the budget allocations to defence were artificially raised by the inclusion of associated items previously listed elsewhere in the budget. This would have served partly as a reassurance for the domestic audience and partly as an indication of Soviet preparedness and resolution. (It is significant that Khrushchev's announcement followed closely President Kennedy's speech reporting a fairly large increase in American defence spending.) If this is so, then likely transfers might have involved defence stockpiling or investments in defence industries. It is also feasible that some procurement for the space programme is now counted as defence expenditure.

By 1964 the sum voted for direct defence spending in the Soviet Union had risen to just over 75 per cent of the US equivalent, compared with 60 per cent in 1960. If part of this increase can be accounted for by the widening of the scope of the Soviet defence vote, then Soviet outlays are probably now about two-thirds of the US level.

Soviet and American Defence Research and Development

The Soviet authorities have never published figures of expenditure on defence research and development. So it is even more difficult to assess the extent of activities in those spheres than it is in the case of direct defence activity. The only figures available are expenditures through the budget on 'science' under the Social and Cultural Vote, and extra-budgetary scientific expenditure. In some years budgetary and extra-budgetary figures are shown separately and in others only as a combined total—a reticence designed to minimise the amount of information available. The table which follows gives the Soviet figures of 'science' expenditure and the summary figures for American expenditure on military research and development. the National Aeronautics and Space Administration (NASA) and on the Atomic Energy Commission.

Year	USSR Outlay on 'Science'			USA			
	Budget	Other	Total	Defence R & D Old Classi-fication	New Classi-fication	NASA	Atomic Energy Pro-gramme
	(Million Roubles)				(Million Dollars)		
1950	540	360	900	871		54*	778
1951	540	...	...	1,063		62*	897
1952	560	...	...	1,565		67*	1,670
1953	630	500	1,130	1,830		78*	1,791
1954	685	...	...	1,806		89*	1,895
1955	830	...	...	1,804	2,630	74*	1,857
1956	1,030	700	1,730	2,202	2,639	71*	1,651
1957	1,360	...	...	2,596	3,371	76	1,990
1958	1,700	720	2,420	2,988	3,664	89	2,268
1959	2,000	820	2,820		4,183	145	2,541
1960	2,340	950	3,290		5,654	401	2,623
1961	2,680	1 120	3,800		6,131	744	2,713
1962	...	...	4,300		6,319	1,257	2,806
1963	...	...	4,700†		6,599†	2,400†	2,870†
1964	...	...	5,200†		7,120†	4,200†	2,850†

* National Advisory Committee for Aeronautics. Much of this expenditure was for aircraft in early years.
† Budget estimate.

The figures for US defence research and development up to 1955 exclude the cost of a good deal of such activity which was financed as procurement of equipment by the armed forces. From 1955 onwards, most of this is shown where it really belongs—in the category of defence research and development proper—hence the recent growth in this category is somewhat exaggerated. On the other hand, the reorganization of the National Advisory Committee for Aeronautics in the National Aeronautics and Space Administration (NASA) has had the opposite effect. Before 1958, virtually the whole cost of the space research programme was shared between the army, navy and air force. Since then, the expenditure of NASA has risen very fast, partly because of transfers from Defence Research and Development.

It is probable that the bulk, if not the whole, of Soviet defence research and development is financed through the budget and through the other allocations shown as being devoted to 'science' outside the scope of the budget. There would appear to be little need to assume that, apart from the atomic energy programme, the authorities have deliberately hidden large amounts of it elsewhere. This conclusion is based on the vast size of the published expenditure on 'science' and on the similarity of its behaviour to that of American defence research and development figures. Thus, between 1956 and 1962, both increased 2.7 times, both having previously been fairly stable for several years. Examination of expenditure by the Atomic Energy Commission shows not only the high cost of the whole programme, but the relatively small proportion accounted for by research and development. The chief components in the US atomic energy total are the outlays on materials and weapons.

In the USSR there is believed to be a special ministry which is responsible for atomic energy, going under the deceptive title of Ministry of Medium Machine Building. Ministries for individual industries were abolished in 1957, but this ministry continues to operate and there are no companion ministries for heavy or light engineering. These somewhat unusual circumstances support the view that the Ministry of Medium Machine Building is the Soviet equivalent of America's Atomic Energy Commission. It is also probable that, enjoying the title that it does, the ministry is financed largely, if not entirely, by a separate vote and not under the general heading of 'science.' This seems all the more probable when it is considered that most of its activity is no more likely to be of the nature of scientific research than is that of the US Atomic Energy Commission; the bulk of the expenditure must involve industrial processes and it would not be surprising if the Soviet authorities financed it through the National Economy Vote. Unfortunately, this Vote is no more revealing than those for defence and science.

Because it is so difficult to compare the size of the Soviet and the American defence research and development and atomic energy programmes, a not unreasonable approach is to proceed from the assumption that the USSR would, if it could, carry out as much, if not more, military, nuclear and space research and development as the USA. Such an assumption does not necessarily derive from pre-conceptions about the malicious intentions of the USSR, but from its own repeated admissions that it feels compelled as a matter of prudence to compete with and outdo the USA in these spheres. In the case of certain important types of guided and ballistic missile and space vehicles, Soviet claims to be doing just this are frequent and are generally acknowledged. What, then, would it cost the USSR to match the American military research and development and space programmes? This question can only be answered by applying the correct rouble/dollar ratio to the American figures. For the most recent period, this may have been the equivalent of 0.44 roubles per dollar.[1] This gives the following rouble equivalents for US expenditure. The Soviet figures of 'science' expenditure are also shown.

	USA	USSR
	(Thousand Million Roubles)	
	*Military R & D and Space Programme**	*Total 'Science' Outlay*
1960	2.66	3.29
1962	3.33	4.30

* Excluding research and development work financed as military procurement. It is not unlikely that Soviet military procurement also contains certain research and development expenditure.

If the correct rouble/dollar ratio has been applied, the US military research and development programme absorbs the rouble equivalent of about 80 per cent of the total Soviet expenditure on 'science', a category known to cover the financing of most military and civil research and development. This suggests that, by applying only modest sums to research and development in non-military spheres, excluding space research, the USSR could match the American programme for research and development for military and space purposes. But Soviet industry is expanding fast, and much research work is known to be in progress in this sphere, as, for example, in

[1] According to the US Joint Economic Committee the ratio in the sphere of research and development was 0.4 roubles per dollar using Soviet weights and 0.6 using American weights which gives a geometric mean of 0.49. The year was 1955, but between then and 1960 US costs must have risen faster than Soviet, justifying the use of 0.44 for 1960. Since 1960, US costs have been more stable, so the same ratio is used for 1962.

petro-chemicals, plastics, and a wide range of other primarily civil research projects. It would, therefore, be unrealistic to assume that Soviet defence and space research and development are as well equipped with funds as in the USA. Examination of the data in the one department on which published information appears to be readily available for both countries supports the view that the USA is likely to be spending more than the USSR on military and space research and development. The department in question is that concerned with missiles and outer space, and the approach is to examine the achievements of both countries as indicated by the firings publicly recorded.

By the middle of 1964 the USA had carried out some 240 space operations, including five probes towards the moon, one planetary probe and four manned vehicles. These were recovered after three to twenty-two orbits of the earth. By the same date the USSR had carried out some seventy-six space operations, including four probes towards the moon, three planetary probes and six manned space vehicles. These were recovered after one to eighty-two orbits of the earth. The USSR had a lead in the weight of payloads put into orbit around the earth, since each of their manned vehicles weighed about 10,500 lbs while those of the USA weighed about 3,000 lbs. The USA is, however, making great efforts to overtake the Soviet lead and has reached an advanced stage in the development of rockets capable of putting 22,000 lbs into orbit and is aiming to increase this weight considerably. The US space programme has always appeared to be more extensive than that of the USSR and more advanced in the costly department of instrumentation.

By the middle of 1964 the Americans had completed the deployment of ICBM's of the first generation and had started to deploy ICBM's of the second generation. Missiles with a range of 1,500 miles which had been deployed in Europe as an interim measure were withdrawn from service. No information is available about missile programmes in the USSR, but much the same could be true here as is known to be true in the case of space vehicles and earth satellites. An estimate of the balance of missile forces between the Western Alliance and the Soviet bloc was published by the British Institute for Strategic Studies in November, 1963. This suggested that missiles operationally available to the West included 475 of intercontinental range and about 200 with a range of about 1,500 miles to be launched from submarines. Figures for the Soviet bloc included over 100 missiles of intercontinental range, some of which were of a second generation with more powerful boosters and larger warheads than their American counterparts, and 800 missiles with ranges between 600 and 2,100 miles. A more recent comparison between the strategic forces of the USA and the USSR was given in August 1964 by the American Secretary of Defense. He stated that the USA had more than 800 ICBM's, mainly deployed in hardened silos, whereas the USSR had under 200 deployed, some of which were in hardened silos. He also claimed that the USA had 256 Polaris missiles deployed in sixteen nuclear-powered submarines, while the USSR had 142 missiles with a range far shorter than that of Polaris, mostly deployed in non-nuclear submarines which could not fire while submerged. If well founded, these estimates would mean a Soviet lead in weapons against Western Europe and an American lead in weapons against the Soviet Union.

The account of space operations bears out the impression that, as a country considerably less powerful than the USA, the USSR is generally satisfied with less complex apparatus and equipment than the USA and is more inclined to concentrate on relatively few projects, whereas the USA can afford to invest in a great diversity of programmes. All this points to a somewhat less expensive Soviet military and space research and development programme, although the great progress made by the USSR suggests that the difference cannot be enormous. The USSR is probably spending about 80 per cent of what is being spent by the USA. This may also be true of the atomic energy programme, about which the available data are even more unsatisfactory than they are in the case of military and space research and development proper.

BIBLIOGRAPHY

The following list of sources is additional to the books and articles referred to in the text of this book.

STATISTICAL COMPENDIUMS

Narodnoye Khozyaistvo SSSR v 1962 (Moscow 1963)
SSSR v Tsifrakh v 1963 (Moscow 1964)
Selskoe Khozyaistvo SSSR (Moscow 1960)
Kapital 'noye Stroitel'stvo (Moscow 1961)
FAO Production Yearbook 1962 (Rome 1962)
UN Statistical Yearbook 1962 (New York 1962)
UN Monthly Bulletin of Statistics (Statistical Office of the UN)
UK Annual Abstract of Statistics 1962
Statistical Abstracts of the USA: 1963 (Washington 1963)
The Budget of the US Government (Annual)
UK Army, Navy and Air Estimates (Annual)
UK Ministry of Defence Estimates (Annual)

OTHER BOOKS

Target Figures for the Economic Development of the Soviet Union. Soviet
    Booklet No. 47 (London 1959)
Report to the 22nd Congress of CPSU by N. S. Khrushchev. Soviet Booklet
    No. 80 (London 1961)
Report on the Programme of the CPSU. Soviet Booklet No. 81 (London 1961)
Joint Economic Committee of the US Congress:
    (a) Comparisons of the US and Soviet Economies (3 vols) (Washington 1959)
    (b) Dimensions of Soviet Economic Power (Washington 1962)
The Soviet Economy. A. Nove (London 1961)
The Soviet Seven Year Plan, with an introduction by A. Nove (London 1960)
Communist Economic Strategy. A. Nove (NPA Washington 1959)
Comparative National Products and Price Levels (OEEC)
Russia's Soviet Economy. H. Schwartz (New York 1950)
An Index of Soviet Industrial Output. N. Kaplan and R. Moorsteen (American
    Economic Review, June 1960)
Soviet Economic Warfare. R. Allen (1960)
Soviet Economic Growth. A. Bergson (ed.) (Evanston 1953)
Soviet Industrial Expansion. F. Seton (Manchester Statistical Society Paper 1957)
The Red Executive. D. Granick (New York 1960)
The Soviet 1956 Statistical Handbook: A Commentary. N. Jasny (East Lansing
    1957)
The Socialized Agriculture of the USSR. N. Jasny (Stanford 1949)

INDEX

Afghanistan, receipt of foreign aid, 128–9, 133; trade with Communist bloc, 122, 123, 126

Agriculture, administrative changes in USSR, 82; Chinese, 102–7, 112–14, 116–17; drop in Soviet output, 26; East-European, 93–5; fertilizers in USSR, 80, 83; gross output in USSR, 84; irrigation in China, 10; irrigation in USSR, 83; labour forces in USA and USSR, 18, 25; maize programme in USSR, 83; output in USSR, 79, 81; problems under Communism, 46; producer co-operatives, 104; Soviet investments in, 78, 79, 82; Soviet labour productivity plans, 78, 80; Soviet Sixth Five Year Plan, 78; Soviet Seven Year Plan, 77–84; US and Soviet output per head, 26

Aid to uncommitted countries, Chinese, 34; comparison of Communist and non-Communist, 35; comparison with defence expenditure, 35; Soviet, 29, 127–35; US, NATO and Japanese, 35, 127–35

Albania, industrial output, 91

Aluminium, Soviet exports, 125

Argentina, aid agreement with Czechoslovakia, 128

Armaments, expenditure on, 29–34, 147–63; output in Soviet Union, 29–34, 67, 138

Asia, expectation of life in, 20; output of, 16

Automation, comparison of Soviet and Western progress with, 56–7; Soviet interest in, 55, 137

Bonus system (*see* Production bonuses)

Building and building materials in the USSR, 74–5

Bulgaria, industrial output, 91; fall in real wages, 93

Burying capitalism, 10, 119

Calbe, 93

Cement, Chinese output, 106; East European output, 91; in USSR, 75

Chemical fibres, Soviet output, 72

Chemical industry of USSR, automation of, 57; investments, 74; output, 72; progress, 70–4, 138

Cherepovets steelworks, 43–4

China, aid to other countries, 129, 131, 133, 135; collective farming in, 102; collectivization, 102, 104, 105, 107, 117; communes, 108, 109, 110; economic backwardness of, 17–18; food shortages, 112, 115; foreign trade, 115–16; great leap forward, 43, 108–14, 117–18; industrial output, 106, 109, 116; industrialization, 105; irrigation, 107; land reform, 104; Mutual Aid Groups, 104; producer co-operatives, 104; Soviet credits to, 105, 132; technical aid from USSR, 105; unemployment, 116; UNRRA aid, 101

Chinese communes, 108, 109, 110

Coal, Chinese output, 106, 109; in Eastern Europe, 91; in USSR, 60–1, 137

Cobalt, Soviet prices, 45

Collective farming, East Germany's problems, 47, 95; in China, 102, 104, 105, 107, 117; incomes in USSR, 82; Polish abandonment of, 47, 96

Colombo plan, 128

Communist area and population, 13; economic backwardness, 17

Consumer goods in USSR, 69, 75–6

Copper, Soviet prices, 44; Soviet output, 76, 81

Council of Mutual Economic Assistance (CMEA), as reply to Marshall Plan, 97; formation of, 120; International Bank, 98; Roumanian resistance to. 98

Credits, Soviet to China, 105; Soviet to underdeveloped countries, 130–5;

For Product Safety Concerns and Information please contact our EU
representative GPSR@taylorandfrancis.com
Taylor & Francis Verlag GmbH, Kaufingerstraße 24, 80331 München, Germany

www.ingramcontent.com/pod-product-compliance
Ingram Content Group UK Ltd.
Pitfield, Milton Keynes, MK11 3LW, UK
UKHW021827240425
457818UK00006B/100

*9 7 8 1 0 3 2 4 9 3 3 4 3 *